The Teacher's Guide
to Flexible Interviewing
in the Classroom

The Teacher's Guide to Flexible Interviewing in the Classroom

LEARNING WHAT CHILDREN KNOW ABOUT MATH

▲ **Herbert P. Ginsburg**
Teachers College, Columbia University

▲ **Susan F. Jacobs**
Manhattanville College

▲ **Luz Stella Lopez**
Marymount School, Colombia, S.A.

Allyn and Bacon
Boston • London • Toronto • Sydney • Tokyo • Singapore

Series editor: Frances Helland
Series editorial assistant: Kris Lamarre
Manufacturing buyer: Megan Cochran

Copyright © 1998 by Allyn & Bacon
A Viacom Company
Needham Heights, MA 02194

Internet: www.abacon.com
America Online: keyword: College Online

Library of Congress Cataloging-in-Publication Data

Ginsburg, Herbert.
    The teacher's guide to flexible interviewing in the classroom :
learning what children know about math / Herbert P. Ginsburg, Susan
F. Jacobs, Luz Stella Lopez.
      p. cm.
    Includes bibliographical references and index.
    ISBN 0-205-26567-7
    1. Mathematics—Study and teaching (Elementary)—Evaluation.
2. Questioning. I. Jacobs, Susan F. II. Lopez, Luz Stella.
III. Title.
QA135.5.G523   1998
372.7'044—dc21   97-38148
                                               CIP

Printed in the United States of America
10 9 8 7 6 5 4 3 2 1   02 01 00 99 98

▲ Contents

CHAPTER EIGHT

What Teachers Say about Using Flexible Interviewing in the Classroom   195

. . . for many teachers, the surest and most direct means for judging the intelligence of a child is to put questions to him, to make him talk. In the class one questions him in such a way as to solicit a personal reply, a reply which does not come from the book. . . . Freed from the constraint of the class, certain minds open, and thus one makes unexpected discoveries . . . it is the spontaneous reflections of the child which indicate his intelligence.

BINET & SIMON,
The Development of Intelligence in Children

▲ *Preface*

The essence of teaching is knowing what individual children think, believe, and know or fail to know. To teach effectively, you need to understand what a child means when she says that two rows of objects "both have the mostest," or why a child believes that "you can't take a big number from a small one." To teach effectively, you need to discover what the shy child really is thinking or why the student from a different culture refuses to answer a question. Curriculum improvements such as the introduction of manipulatives or computers will not be truly effective unless teachers understand how children think and what children know. Unfortunately, helping teachers to gain insight into children's minds is often a key missing link in educational reform.

How can teachers achieve such understanding? Traditional standardized tests are of limited value in accomplishing this goal. The Standards of the National Council of Teachers of Mathematics urge teachers to go in new directions, and particularly to conduct more "authentic" assessments of students. But teachers need more help than they now receive in order to perform the kind of assessment recommended by the Standards.

This book helps teachers to understand and use one essential form of assessment aimed at uncovering children's thinking about mathematics (and other subjects, too)—the flexible interview. Although it is now achieving some popularity as the field of education emphasizes authentic assessment, the flexible interview remains poorly understood. In a sense, there is nothing very new about flexible interviewing. Indeed, good teachers have always used something like it. For them, engaging in informal conversation with students to understand their thinking has always been part and parcel of good teaching.

In recent years, however, particularly through the work of Piaget, the flexible interview has been elaborated and developed. It is now an extremely powerful tool for investigating children's thinking. The flexible interview is more than an informal conversation that can be conducted in a casual manner. To use the flexible interview effectively, teachers need to acquire a deeper understanding of its rationale and need to learn how it can be used both in conjunction with and in the service of classroom instruction.

Our goal is to help elementary-level teachers and students of elementary education to understand and use flexible interviewing. In this book, which requires no special background in mathematics education or psychology, we describe practical ways of using flexible interviews in the classroom to learn what children know about mathematics (and other subjects) and to teach them more effectively. The methods we describe, based on Piaget's "constructivist" approach, were developed and tested by classroom teachers with whom we worked. Although the focus is on mathematics, the relevance is broader—the flexible interview can be used in connection with children's learning of almost any school subject.

Chapter 1 begins by describing both the strengths and the limitations of standard tests. Then it uses an extended example to describe the essence of the flexible interview and the rationale for it. The chapter concludes by describing the experiment we conducted with teachers to learn how the flexible interview can be used under ordinary classroom conditions.

Chapter 2 discusses how teachers can learn to prepare children for work with interviewing, to create a classroom atmosphere conducive to conducting interviews, and to manage a classroom in which interviewing is a regular occurrence.

Chapter 3 shows how teachers can use several techniques to conduct interviews with individual children in their classrooms.

Chapter 4 describes several ways in which teachers can conduct interviews with groups of children as part of regular classroom activities.

Chapter 5 presents the story of an unusual, and successful, experiment in which one of our teachers taught her second graders to interview one another. This chapter describes the techniques she used.

Chapter 6 presents general guidelines for using the flexible interview. The chapter describes such issues as how to prepare for interviews, how to motivate children, how to probe for thinking processes, and how to establish children's competence. This chapter is not a cookbook but a set of practical principles and rules.

Chapter 7 presents specific questions that teachers may use as the basis for flexible interviews. Organized by "big ideas" in mathematics, the questions cover *major* topics—not all topics—of the mathematics curriculum from grades K through 5.

Finally, Chapter 8 describes how our volunteer teachers evaluated their experiences using the various interview methods that they created. Interviewing helped them to see children in new ways and to improve their teaching. We think that this is what can happen for you too.

Our appreciation goes to the following reviewers for their comments on the manuscript: Jeanne Reardon, Montgomery County Public Schools and Carol McKneely, Caddo Middle Magnet School.

We are indebted to the National Science Foundation, which supported our work with a grant (TPE-9053556). We thank Cambridge University Press for permission to use some material from Ginsburg's *Entering the Child's Mind: The Clinical Interview in Psychological Research and Practice.* But most of all, we are grateful to the teachers and administrators who collaborated with us and supported our work:

From PS 87 in Manhattan: Jane Hand, Karen Mantlo, Trudy Orgas, Mellisande Schwartzfarb, Margot Solberg, and Caroline Svesko.

From the Fieldston Lower School in Riverdale: Joyce Baron, Mary Neale, David Smelin, Harry Sunshine, and Fredda Tick.

From New Canaan Country School: Lilani Balasuriya, Sandy Burn, Loretta Gilson, Antoinette Heffner, Barbara Kutner, Kiki Sweigert, and Mary Whitman.

From the Chatsworth School in Mamaroneck: Joan Gansfuss, Carole Garinger, Kay Kobbe, Michael Rainaldi, and Nancy Stamegna.

Thanks to you all!

CHAPTER ONE

▲ *What Is Flexible Interviewing and Why Should You Use It?*

This chapter covers three topics. First, we discuss why standard tests—classroom tests or end-of-the-year achievement tests—are of limited value for classroom teachers. In general, tests do not provide the kind of information that can help teachers teach. Tests may show how well a child is performing, but they yield little insight into how the child thinks, why the child fails to learn, or what can be done to help the child learn.

The National Council of Teachers of Mathematics (NCTM; 1995) proposes that, because of the limitations of tests, teachers need to engage in "alternative" or "authentic" forms of assessment. The focus of both assessment and teaching, NCTM argues, should be children's mathematical minds, not simply right and wrong answers. The second part of this chapter discusses one form of alternative assessment, the flexible interview, which we believe to be an extremely powerful technique for understanding how children think and learn. Using an extended example, we describe the basic features of the flexible interview. We explain how it can provide insight into children's thinking, into their errors and unsuspected strengths, and into their underlying competence. We argue that the information gained from the flexible interview can help you teach more effectively. You should use it in your classroom.

But that is easier said than done. How is it possible to interview effectively when you are required to deal with some twenty or thirty children in a bustling classroom? How can you integrate it into your teaching? How can you find the time to do it? Do you need extensive training to do it well? Initially, we did not know the answers to these questions, so we tried to find out by experimenting in schools. The third part of this chapter describes how we collaborated with eighteen teachers to develop practical ways to use flexible interviewing in and out of the classroom.

The rest of the book, chapters 2 through 8, describes the results of our joint work—various ways in which teachers can use interviewing in the classroom; guidelines for interviewing; tips about how you can learn to interview; questions that can form the basis for interviews about key mathematical subjects; and, finally, how teachers evaluate their experience with flexible interviews in the classroom.

▲ Some Problems with Standard Tests

Readers of this book will have taken many standard tests throughout their school careers and will probably have a pretty good idea about what these tests are and what is wrong with them. You have taken classroom tests devised by your teachers, tests at the end of chapters in your textbooks, end-of-the-year achievement tests, intelligence tests, aptitude tests, and the like. You know that these tests are "standardized" in the sense that the method of administration must be uniform. Everyone gets the same questions in the same way, with the same time constraints, in the same language, and everyone has an equal chance to respond. In general, standard tests are devised to yield answers that can be scored without controversy—calculational responses, multiple choice, yes–no answers, and other short answers. The correct answers need to be obvious so that they can be scored by machine or at least fairly easily and with good agreement by human judges. So the essence of the standard test is uniform administration—everyone gets the same test in the same way—and ease of scoring.

Though flawed in various ways, standard tests were developed for good reasons. Indeed, one of the motivations for them was ethical. As far back as 1845, Horace Mann offered several reasons for introducing standardized tests to the schools (Wainer, 1992):

> They are impartial.
> They are just to the pupils.
> They prevent the officious interference of the teacher.
> They take away all possibility of favoritism.

They make the information obtained available to all.
They enable all to appraise the ease or difficulty of the questions. (p. 15)

In one way or another, these reasons revolve around *fairness* or impartiality. Thus, one justification is that standard tests prevent the teacher from favoring some children over others (perhaps by giving some children easier questions than others) or from interfering with the process of testing. Another justification is that the tests make the process public, so that an outside observer can see whether the questions were too hard or too easy.

The method for achieving this kind of fairness is to treat all students alike, to give everyone the same conditions for running the race. From this point of view, no one should be given easier questions than anyone else; no person should be judged on a different basis from another. A wrong answer should be a wrong answer for all.

So there was noble motivation for developing the method of standardized testing. Indeed, the method can produce some useful information for the classroom teacher. If it is successful, the standard test can describe, with reasonable accuracy and fairness, whether a child's performance has improved over time and how well a child performs compared with peers. Suppose that Kim correctly answers almost all problems on a classroom test of addition that you have devised. You may learn from these results that she is now able to solve two-digit addition problems with regrouping, whereas she was not able to do so before, and you may also be pleased to learn that her performance is at about the same level as her peers'. All of this is useful information, and the standard test is a reasonable method for getting it.

But there are many problems with standard testing. Chief among them is the fact that poor performance is very difficult to interpret. Some children misunderstand standard test questions; some are not motivated to take the test; others make trivial mistakes that lead to incorrect responses. In all these cases, low test scores do not necessarily indicate a real lack of ability. The scores show that the child performed badly, but they do not conclusively demonstrate that the cause was a lack of understanding or knowledge.

Consider this example: Jill has been given a standard test problem in which she had to determine how much change would be left over from a dollar if she bought two dozen eggs at 45¢ a dozen. Her answer was 20¢.

I: Say out loud how you did it.

J: Since it was 45¢ for one dozen and 45¢ for the other, and 45 and 45 is 80, so 80 from 100 or a dollar is 20¢.

I: So you said 45 and 45 is . . . ?

J: 80 . . . [She hesitates, drawing out the word *eighty,* and looks very unsure.]

I: Are you sure?

J: No, 90.

I: So the answer is?

J: 10.

In this case, the questioning revealed that her strategy was sensible: she knew that she had to add up the two amounts and subtract the sum from the total to get the answer. The only faulty part of her procedure was the number fact: she believed that 45 + 45 = 80 (which she did, in fact, subtract correctly from 100). But the incorrect number fact resulted from mere sloppiness. When given the chance to reconsider the number fact answer, she spontaneously corrected it and then completed the problem correctly. Clearly, her analysis of the problem was correct, her procedures were mostly correct, and the minor flaw in her recall was easily corrected.

Success on the test may also be deceptive. Most people have had the experience of getting through a test, indeed even doing well on it, without understanding much of the material. Just as a wrong answer may not indicate a lack of understanding, so a right answer may not indicate the presence of understanding.

Here is an example: Dorothy was told, "Listen carefully and tell me if the sentence I say is a good or bad sentence: 'Tom's sister haven't been shopping today.' " She replied, "Bad sentence." The interviewer asked, "Why?" Dorothy replied: "Because they didn't have food to eat for dinner." In other words, Dorothy seemed to think that the sentence was bad not because it was grammatically incorrect, but because it would lead to an unfortunate result—namely, nothing to eat for dinner.

We see, then, that tests deal with *performance,* with right and wrong answers, but that they typically fail to provide clear information concerning underlying *knowledge* or *thinking.* Correct answers to test items may not indicate the presence of understanding, and wrong answers may not indicate its absence.

It is even possible to argue that tests may discourage children from employing rich thought. Interesting, complex thinking generally does not take place in a short period of time in response to a narrowly focused test item. Indeed, children may learn *not* to think—or not to think deeply—in response to test items. Too much thought might lead a child to believe that none of the four multiple-choice answers is really correct, that the question was not very good in the first place, and that another issue is really involved. If the child tries to work all this out, he or she will not have enough time to get the (wrong) right answer that produces credit on the test.

What does this mean for you as a teacher? What use can you make of standardized tests? They may perform a valuable function in helping you to learn about children's levels of performance. You may not have realized that Noriyuki is now capable of doing double digit multiplication, or that Annie has difficulty with subtraction problems involving regrouping. But that is only a beginning. You need to discover whether Noriyuki really understands the multiplication problems that he can solve. Perhaps he just uses the computational procedure blindly and mechanically and doesn't understand anything about why it is used or when to use it. You need to find out why Annie is not able to solve these particular kinds of subtraction problems. Does she have trouble with the number facts, with "borrowing," or with basic concepts of place value?

Getting the answers to these questions will help you in your most important goal, developing strategies for helping both Noriyuki and Annie. What is the next step for Noriyuki if he does not really comprehend multiplication? How can Annie be helped to master subtraction with regrouping? If you can gain insight into the thinking of Noriyuki and Annie, into what they understand and misunderstand, into what strategies they employ, then you can teach them more effectively.

But standard tests are not designed to provide the sorts of information most useful for teaching. At their best, standardized tests—the classroom tests you construct, the tests provided by the textbooks, and the national or state achievement tests—can portray a child's level of performance—for example, whether a child is performing better than before, or at the level of peers. Typically, standardized tests provide little information concerning the knowledge or thinking that underlies the child's response. If you do not have this insight, you will not understand why a child is having trouble learning mathematics; you will not appreciate how a child arrives at an answer; and your teaching will not be as effective as it could be. That is why we need alternative forms of assessment, particularly the flexible interview, which can provide fascinating insights into children's thinking.

▲ *Interviewing Jennifer*

The flexible interview is both old and new. On the one hand, good teachers have always talked with students to discover something about their thinking and learning. At least from the time of Socrates, teachers have engaged in dialogue with students to find out what they think and to help them learn. On the other hand, systematic use of the flexible interview has occurred only in the twentieth century. Jean Piaget, the great Swiss psychologist whose work revolutionized the study of the child, developed flexible interviewing (which he called "clinical" interviewing because he felt it requires clinical sensitivity, not because he was dealing with disturbed children) into a powerful technique with which to examine the processes of thinking. (You can read about his development and use of the method in Ginsburg & Opper, 1988, and Piaget, 1976.)

Whether old or new, the flexible interview deserves careful study. Talking with children is more complicated than it may appear on the surface. We begin by considering an example of an individual child who was interviewed concerning her knowledge of simple arithmetic. We highlight basic features of the method and the kinds of insights it can provide.

At the time of the interview, which took place about two-thirds of the way through the academic year in a relatively quiet room in the school, Jennifer was a first grader. The interviewer (Herbert Ginsburg) was not her teacher. He was an outsider (although a parent of children in the school), conducting the interview in order to obtain videotaped examples of children's mathematical thinking for use in teacher workshops. The goal of the interview was not to help Jennifer with some problem or even to investigate some particular aspect of mathematical thinking. Indeed, the interviewer knew nothing about Jennifer's learning history or level of performance, only that she was a cute and charming little girl who eagerly agreed to participate in the interview and answer the various questions.

Of course it is hard to know what Jennifer thought about the interview at the outset. From the child's point of view, the whole situation must have been highly unusual. The teacher simply told her that she would leave the room to do something interesting, perhaps to "play some games," with "Doctor" Somebody-or-Other, or perhaps with Susie's father. In any event, the purpose of the interview probably was not clear to Jennifer. Furthermore, the situation was made even more strange by the fact that in addition to Jennifer and the interviewer, a video camera operator and another adult were also in the room. Could all these factors conspire to undermine the success of the interview? You can judge for yourself. But it has been our experience that children adjust very easily to the videotaping situation; they get so absorbed in working on the mathematical problems and in the process of interviewing that they seem to forget about the camera and various adults in the room. And of course, if the child's teacher is conducting the interview, many of these problems do not arise.

The interviewer began by showing the child a small stuffed rabbit and squirrel. (The interviewer is designated by H and the child by J.)

> H: Let's see. This is . . .
> J: A rabbit.
> H: A rabbit, O.K. And this is?
> J: A squirrel.

Jennifer appeared to be charmed by the stuffed animals and seemed eager to play with them.

> H: Squirrel, O.K. Now we're going to tell some stories about the squirrel and the rabbit. The rabbit has 3 carrots and the squirrel also likes carrots. And the squirrel, it's kind of a strange squirrel. . . . And the squirrel has 4 carrots.

As the interviewer described the squirrel liking carrots, Jennifer smiled. When the interviewer said that the squirrel was strange, Jennifer laughed and nodded her head as if to agree.

Note that the interviewer did not begin with an obvious, written math problem. Instead he employed a story about a squirrel and a rabbit. The situation was partly concrete in that characters in the story were represented by stuffed animals, and partly abstract in that both animals were said to possess imaginary carrots. There were two reasons for using the story. One was that the interviewer was attempting to put the child at ease—to establish rapport. He wanted to convince her that the interview would be enjoyable, and for a first grader, a story, and especially the stuffed animals, might be better tools than a written math problem for accomplishing this.

Another reason is that flexible interviews often revolve around extended problems. The interviewer does not simply ask, "Tell me what you know about addition," or, "How do you subtract?" Instead, the interviewer attempts to present a particular problem for the child to grapple with. Of course, the nature of the problem should vary according to the age of the child and the child's experience in school. A young child might be asked to add collections of blocks, whereas an older child might be asked to add written numbers or even to do mental addition. In developing the problems, the interviewer needs to take into account the child's developmental level, what the child has been studying in school, and the like. But the important point is to give the child a *problem*—something specific to think about. In Jennifer's case, a combination of concrete objects (the squirrel and rabbit) and imaginary ones (the carrots) seemed to fit the bill.

Next the interviewer decided to check on whether Jennifer had been listening to and understood the problem.

H: So the rabbit has how many?

J: 3.

H: And the squirrel has?

J: 4.

When the child takes a standard test, you usually do not know whether he or she has understood the problem or even remembered the basic points (for example, that the numbers are 3 and 4). You do not know because typically you are not permitted to ask. But in the flexible interview, checks on the child's attention and understanding are not only permitted, but desirable. Why proceed unless you are sure that the child understands the basic problem?

Next, the interviewer posed the problem.

H: How many carrots do they have all together?

At this point Jennifer paused and seemed to be whispering the counting numbers. After a while, she spoke softly.

J: 6.

H: 6. How did you figure that out? I saw that you were counting a little.

Jennifer gave a wrong answer. But note several points concerning the interviewer's response. He did *not* say, "No, you are wrong. The correct answer is 7." Instead, he ignored the incorrectness of the response and asked the fundamental question of the flexible interview: "How did you figure that out?" This question, of course, comes in many forms: "How did you do it?" "How did you get that answer?" "How did you know?" But whatever the form, the purpose is to ask the child to explain what he or she has just done. Sometimes the interviewer can get some of this information just by observing the child. Thus, in this case, the interviewer had seen Jennifer whispering what appeared to be some numbers. Still, he needed more information concerning what exactly the child had done and therefore asked her to describe her method.

J: Right. I, so I like had in my mind a 4 and a 3 and then I, for 4 I put, I moved one of them over to the 4 and that was 5. And the other one over and that was 6.

As Jennifer described what she had in her mind, she pointed to her head. Her statement seemed to indicate that she started with the 4, the larger number, and then moved one from the remaining set (the 3) over to the same mental space occupied by the 4, getting 5, and then moved one more over to get 6.

Several things can be said about this. First, her wrong answer was not simply an incorrect guess or a faulty number fact. Rather, it was the result of a systematic strategy. It was as if she had started with a pile of 4 blocks, moved one more over to get 5, then moved another to get 6. In fact, this is one of the earliest kinds of addition in which preschoolers all over the world engage (Ginsburg, 1989). Her addition strategy could be described as combining sets and then counting the members of the sets to get the sum. Further, she may have been using—although we don't yet have enough evidence to be sure about it—the economical strategy of *counting on from the larger number*. It is easier to count on from 4 than from 3. (In this case, counting from the larger versus the smaller number really doesn't make much difference, but imagine that the child is trying to add 15 + 1.)

After Jennifer got the answer 6, she seemed to be a little puzzled, as if she knew that something was wrong. The interviewer decided on the spot to explore this interpretation. Note that in the flexible interview, the interviewer is constantly engaged in interpreting the child's response and then has the freedom to develop questions that might shed light on the interpretation. Another way of saying this is that the interviewer theorizes and collects evidence to check the theory.

> *H: Is there anything left?*
> *J: Yeah. 7.*

As she said this, Jennifer looked up in the air as if she noticed that one imaginary carrot had not been counted. She then seemed to correct her earlier omission of this carrot by adding it to the total, and in this way got the right answer to the problem.

> *H: O.K. So you pictured them. You have a little picture in your mind of these carrots. You kind of moved them together. Oh, that's very good.*
> *J: Like a puzzle.*

Jennifer seemed to agree with the interviewer's interpretation and remarked that the problem was like a puzzle, which might have meant that it involved moving (imaginary) pieces into their proper positions to get a satisfying and correct result.

At this point, the interviewer knew that despite the initial wrong answer, Jennifer seemed to be a bright girl who thought intelligently about the simple addition problem. She used a strategy that seemed to indicate some basic understanding of addition. At the same time, she did not implement the strategy correctly. Given this information, the interviewer decided to give Jennifer some similar problems in order to check the generality of the results and the validity of the interpretations reached to this point.

> *H: Like a puzzle. O.K. Let's do another game like that. O.K. Now let's make believe that the squirrel has 6 carrots. Strange that squirrel likes carrots.*
> *J: Yeah.*

In saying this, Jennifer again smiled and looked amused.

> *H: Yeah. And rabbit wants to get 3 carrots. O.K. So squirrel is gonna give rabbit 3 carrots. How many carrots does squirrel have left?*

This time, Jennifer did not ponder the question for any length of time. She responded immediately.

J: 3.

H: 3. How did you know that?

J: Well, I know, well, I know that 3 and 3 is 6. And so, and so I know if I take 3 away from 6 you have 3 left.

Now this is interesting and also a bit surprising. In response to the fundamental question ("How did you know that?"), Jennifer revealed the use of another strategy, which might be described as reasoning from the inverse. Her argument was basically that if it is true that 3 + 3 is 6, then it also must be true, because subtraction is the inverse of addition, that 6 − 3 is 3. Of course, she did not make her argument in exactly those words, and she was not conscious of the axiom that subtraction is the inverse of addition. But she seemed to know all this at an informal, *intuitive* level. Note too that the strategy employed on this problem was different from the one she used in the first problem, namely counting on from the larger number.

At this point, the interviewer was fascinated with Jennifer's performance and wondered what she might do next on another subtraction problem. As you will see, the result was intriguing.

H: Oh, very good. Very good. Let's try another one. Rabbit has 7 carrots and he gives 2 of them to squirrel. How many carrots does rabbit have left?

J: 4.

Jennifer said this softly, as if asking a question, perhaps a bit unsure of her response. If you are counting right and wrong answers, you will note that she is now wrong on two out of three problems.

H: O.K. How did you figure that out?

J: I did the same thing.

H: Same thing. Tell me about it.

Again the interviewer asked the fundamental question to learn how she solved the problem.

J: Well, I knew that 4 and 2 is 7. And if rabbit has 7 carrots and he wants to share them with squirrel, so he gives squirrel 2. He must have 4 left.

Jennifer's line of reasoning was remarkable. She began with an incorrect number fact, 4 + 2 = 7. But given that faulty assumption, her logic was impeccable. If 4 + 2 = 7, then it must be true that 7 − 2 = 4, because subtraction is the inverse of addition. Moreover, just as she understood that addition involves combining sets, so she realized that subtraction means partitioning them: rabbit would have to give a subset to squirrel and would then have a certain amount as the remainder.

Clearly, Jennifer was not simply guessing. Her incorrect response—she now was wrong on two out of three!—was not the result of stupidity, limited memory, a low IQ, or poor mathematical aptitude. Her answer was indeed wrong, but it was the result of an interesting reasoning process and sound, though intuitive, concepts of addition, subtraction, and the inverse relation between them. Psychologists, following Piaget (1973), would say that her answer was produced by an "invented" or "constructed" strategy (Ginsburg & Baron, 1992). Drawing on her experiences with numbers, Jennifer developed her own way of thinking about addition and subtraction. She defined addition and subtraction in her own terms, one of which was her belief that 4 + 2 = 7.

This is the main reason that you should use flexible interviewing. To understand children's performance in math, you need to look beneath the surface. You need to find out the meaning of a wrong answer—and of a correct one, too. You need to see that a wrong answer may not necessarily indicate a lack of knowledge. Indeed, it may have been produced by rather sophisticated understanding and strategy, as was true of Jennifer's 7 − 4 = 2. Standard tests seldom allow you to do this. The flexible interview is the primary instrument for accomplishing this purpose.

Moreover, the flexible interview can suggest ways of helping the child move forward. Although Jennifer seemed to have a good understanding of the concepts and reasonable calculational strategies, she did of course get wrong answers, and so it was the adult's responsibility to help her do better.

How might this be done? Suppose that all you knew—perhaps from a classroom test—is that Jennifer was wrong on the problem 7 − 2 = 5. One approach might have been simply to tell Jennifer that she was wrong and to inform her—repeatedly—of the correct answer. She could be given drill on subtraction problems like this, and one of the cards to be flashed frequently would be 7 − 2 = 5. This is what is sometimes affectionately referred to as the "drill-and-kill" approach, and it is the traditional method of mathematics education.

This might have worked, in the sense that Jennifer would eventually *say* that 7 – 2 = 5, but from a constructivist point of view this type of drill is not a productive approach, for several reasons. One is that Jennifer, not understanding *why* 7– 2 = 5, might simply parrot whatever the adult says and not learn anything important. A second reason is that her problem was not really the failure to remember the correct answer to 7 – 2. Instead, the real problem was that she did not know the answer to 4 + 2. The standard test could not give you that information. Indeed, you would not have identified Jennifer's real problem unless you asked her how she knew that 7 – 2 = 4 —unless you interviewed her in a flexible manner.

How then to help Jennifer? Just drill her on 4 + 2? No: this too would be only mindless memorization. From a constructivist point of view, Jennifer would benefit more from having to construct a new understanding of 4 + 2 and how she could then use her existing knowledge of the inverse relation between addition and subtraction to solve the problem. Here is what the interviewer did.

> *H: Right. O.K. Very good. How could you make sure that you're really right about that? You said that 7 take away 2 was 4, right? Because 4 and 2 is 7. O.K. Could you show me with the blocks that 4 and 2 is 7?*

The interviewer's strategy was not to tell Jennifer that 4 + 2 = 6 but to have her figure it out herself by using real objects. Immediately, Jennifer again defined the problem in her own terms. Instead of dealing with the problem suggested by the interviewer, she decided to figure out the answer to 7 – 2.

> *J: O.K. First let me get 7 blocks.*
> *H: O.K. Good idea.*
> *J: 1, 2, 3, 4, 5, 6, 7. O.K.*

Jennifer then removed two blocks from the pile of 7.

> *J: So there's 2 over here.*
> *H: So you did take away 2, right? So how many are left?*

At this point Jennifer, apparently realizing that something was wrong, counted the blocks. She had expected that the answer would be 4, but there were obviously more than that in front of her. She knew this because she had placed 4 blocks in a square and saw that there was one left over. She paused.

J: Wait. Let me count these again.
H: O.K.

She counted.

J: O.K. So it's 5.
H: So 7 take away 2 is . . .
J: 5.
H: And you could show me with those blocks.
J: Right.
H: O.K. Very good.

The interviewer had placed Jennifer in a situation of conflict. (See Baroody, in press, for an interesting discussion of the role of conflict situations in teaching.) Her reasoning told her that $7 - 2 = 4$, but the experiment with blocks told her that $7 - 2 = 5$. Working with the blocks seemed to make a big impression on her and probably was more instructive than simply being told the correct answer. At the same time, she still had much to learn. She needed to retrace her reasoning in the original problem so that she would understand why she had earlier believed that $7 - 2 = 4$, and she needed to deal with her mistaken view about $4 + 2$. But she was off to a good start because the interview had provided insight into why she had made her original mistake.

▲ *The Essence of the Flexible Interview*

As we have seen, a good deal can be accomplished in even a brief interview. Indeed, the episode with Jennifer was only about four minutes long. Now let's summarize some key features of the flexible interview and what can be learned from it.

Presenting the Problem

The interviewer begins by presenting a problem that gives the child something specific to work with. Often, with young children, the problems employ concrete objects. With older children, the problems may involve numbers or even general ideas. But the essence of the matter is that the problems should engage children in active and extended thought that the interview can explore.

Checking Comprehension

The interviewer makes sure that the child understands the basic features of the problem. This can be done by restating the problem, changing the wording, or questioning the child about it. The interviewer enjoys the freedom to make whatever modifications in the problem are necessary and to check on the child's understanding of it. Why continue the interview if the child misunderstands the problem's basic requirements?

Investigating Thought

Once the child gives a response, the interviewer usually wishes to understand the child's thinking. The interviewer does not correct wrong answers. The interviewer usually does not *teach* at this point (although there are exceptions, which will be discussed in later chapters). Instead, the interviewer tries to investigate the thinking that underlies the child's response, whether right or wrong. How did the child solve the problem? What did the child mean by that answer? To find out, the interviewer may ask the fundamental question, which takes many forms: "How did you figure that out?" "How do you know?" "What do you mean?"

Interpreting

Unlike standardized testing, interviewing requires as much thought and effort on the part of the interviewer as on the part of the child. The most important feature of interviewing is interpreting the child's response. Indeed, the response is useless unless you have some idea what it means. Good interviewing is a very thoughtful activity. The interviewer constantly makes hunches about the child's thinking. This is a kind of practical "theorizing" about individual children that good teachers must engage in all the time.

Children's Constructions

The main reason for interviewing is that it can provide insight into the distinctive ways in which children think about—construct—the world of school mathematics. It is not an exaggeration to claim that many teachers do not know what their students understand and how they think. Many teachers have little appreciation of the meaning of wrong answers and hence think that the child has not learned anything, has little mathematics aptitude, or perhaps even suffers from a learning disability. But these interpretations may be wrong. As we have seen in the case of Jennifer, sophisticated reasoning and concepts may underlie wrong answers. Moreover, right answers may simply be rote responses, based on no understanding. The major benefit of flexible interviewing is that it can allow you to "enter the child's mind" (Ginsburg, 1998)—that is, to gain some understanding of children's constructions of mathematics.

Teaching

Of course, you have a practical reason for interviewing—namely, to improve your teaching. By providing specific information concerning the child's understandings, misunderstandings, and methods of solution, the interview allows you to devise strategies for teaching the child more effectively. If you know that despite her wrong answers, Jennifer understands the basic concepts of addition and subtraction and the inverse relation between the two, you have a lot to work with in your attempts to correct her faulty memory for some number facts. Understanding children's thinking allows you to treat them as individuals—to take advantage of their often unsuspected strengths and to identify their real weaknesses.

Understanding Children Who Are Different

A particular strength of the flexible interview is that it can help you to understand children who are different—who are not performing as well as other children, who seem to be learning-disabled, who do not communicate easily, or who are members of minority groups or different cultures. Often it is hard to get to know these children by using conventional methods like standard tests. Under ordinary conditions, these children often perform badly and seem not to know much. But conventional methods may not be suitable for revealing their true competence. You may have a much better chance of getting beyond their poor performance and of finding out what they are really capable of if you employ flexible interviewing. Give them a chance. They may tell you some surprising things that will change your view of them.

▲ *Experimenting with Flexible Interviewing in the Classroom*

Suppose that you are willing to accept that flexible interviewing is a powerful tool that can help you understand your children's thinking and teach more effectively. How can you use this apparently difficult method in your classroom? Is interviewing of this type really practical if you have to deal every day with a class of some twenty or thirty children (or more)? How can interviewing be made a part of everyday classroom activities? How can it be integrated into and thereby improve instruction? How can you get through the math textbook and also have time for interviewing? Can interviewing be done in a group setting? Can you learn to conduct useful interviews without a great deal of special training? How do you come up with the questions to ask? Is interviewing worth the time and energy?

These are all realistic and eminently practical questions, which need to be answered before teachers can engage in flexible interviewing in the classroom. We were often asked questions like these when we conducted workshops designed to help teachers understand children's mathematical thinking. When we showed videotapes of interviews with children like Jennifer, teachers would often comment that the child's thinking was fascinating and that the flexible interview method seemed powerful, but that they did not see how they could possibly use it in their classrooms.

At first, we did not know how to respond to their concerns. Piaget developed the clinical interview method to investigate the thinking of individual children, and that is how psychological researchers use the method. They do not work with groups of children, and in fact they generally do not know much about what goes on in classrooms. For both of these reasons, they cannot provide answers to the teacher's practical questions.

What to do? We felt that the only honest way to find out whether and how flexible interviewing might be used systematically in classrooms was to investigate the matter directly with the collaboration of teachers. We would recruit some teachers to work with us, teach them what we knew about flexible interviewing, and then together develop and evaluate several classroom applications of interviewing.

We went about this experiment in the following way: first, we contacted several teachers and school administrators with whom we had already worked. They were familiar with our approach to studying the development of children's mathematical thinking. In fact, several had already worked with us as students or colleagues in this area. With their aid, we recruited a total of eighteen volunteers who taught at the primary and elementary levels (grades K–4). These teachers were faced with the typical responsibilities of running a full-time classroom throughout the school year. They were not university researchers or employees. In several respects, however, they were not typical: they knew about our work, were interested in flexible interviewing, and volunteered for the project. But, of course, that is why we were interested in collaborating with them.

The teachers worked in four different settings: an inner-city school with a high proportion of African American and Latino students; a middle-class suburban school; and two wealthy private schools (with very few minority students). Each setting presented different challenges. But in all of these settings, the teachers were able to develop and use interesting forms of flexible interviewing. Indeed, we felt that some of the most innovative work took place in the inner-city school.

We began by conducting workshops designed to introduce the volunteer teachers to flexible interviewing with individual children and to explore what it reveals about the development of mathematical thinking. Then we worked with individual teachers to develop forms of interviewing with which they felt most comfortable for use in their classrooms. Some teachers decided to explore interviewing individual children; others worked with groups of children. One teacher was particularly interested in how children might be helped to interview each other. We visited each teacher's classroom about once a week over a period of four or five months, observed what the teachers were up to, made suggestions, videotaped some of their individual and group activities, and discussed their work. We all did our best to develop the activities that they found interesting and felt were promising.

Teachers within schools exchanged ideas, and on several occasions we held meetings for teachers from different schools. Some teachers were particularly talented and threw themselves into the work. Some, we think, did not really believe us when we said at the outset that we did not know how to conduct interviewing in classrooms and would therefore rely on their expertise. They seemed to expect us to tell them what to do and were disappointed, and somewhat at a loss, when we did not. Some teachers contributed more than others, but that is true of any joint endeavor, and all made contributions for which we are grateful. At the end of the project, the teachers took the time to share with us evaluations of their experience. These evaluations and our own impressions are the only "evidence" we collected concerning the success of the project. We have no "objective" measures of the ways in which interviewing improved teaching; we do not know how the use of flexible interviewing affected the children's long-term achievement. That sort of research remains to be done.

The result of the collaboration is that we can describe some very practical ways in which you can conduct flexible interviewing in your classrooms. That is what the rest of this book is all about. Is it hard to learn these methods? Our experience has shown that with a bit of practice you can learn the basics of interviewing in the classroom, and that with further experience you may become adept at it. In any event, you can explore the methods we describe and decide for yourselves whether they are difficult to learn and whether they contribute to your teaching. Please let us know what you find by contacting us on the Internet at **hpg4@columbia.edu.**

_____

CHAPTER TWO

▲ *Preparing Students for the Thinking-Oriented Classroom*

We hope that we have convinced you that clinical interviewing can provide deep insights into children's thinking and learning and that you ought to try interviewing yourself. But before you can get started, you need to prepare students for the experience. This preparation includes the following:

- Developing a classroom atmosphere that encourages the expression of thinking
- Helping students learn to express their thinking

These two aspects of students' preparation are related to each other. An accepting environment enables children to express their thinking. Children need to feel that their thoughts and feelings are valued and respected. Likewise, to talk about their thinking, children need to learn skills such as using a thinking vocabulary, listening to their peers' thinking, reflecting on their thinking, writing about their thinking, and analyzing and evaluating the thinking of their classmates.

There are many ways to prepare students to participate in a thinking-oriented classroom. The ways described in this chapter are based on our experience working with teachers in their classrooms. Through excerpts from actual interviews, we will illustrate how they went about preparing their students. Many of these interviews illustrate the work of Mary, a first-grade teacher at a public school in New York City. The focus of Mary's work was problem solving. Let's look first at a lesson that introduces students to the new vocabulary of thinking.

▲ *Introducing the Vocabulary of Thinking*

Children need to be familiar with terms such as *thinking, strategy, plan, check, represents,* and *prove* before they can begin to talk about what they are thinking and doing. These terms are used routinely in the thinking-oriented classroom. For children to be able to talk about what they are thinking, they need to use expressions like these:

- "I was *thinking* . . . "
- "I *solved* it by . . . "
- "My *strategy* is . . . "
- "I *plan* to use a method that . . . "
- "I *checked* it by . . . "
- "This cube *represents* a . . . "
- "I will *prove* it by . . . "

Teachers should be concerned with the thinking vocabulary in their teaching of any subject matter, not just mathematics. A thinking vocabulary is more than just a tool for flexible interviewing; it is the essence of thoughtful learning.

Knowledge of the vocabulary of thinking does not develop spontaneously. Research has shown that young children typically find it difficult to talk about their thinking. For one thing, mastering the vocabulary with which to communicate their thinking is not easy; even adults have a difficult time coming to an agreement about the definitions of some of these words. Therefore, one of the first steps toward the thinking-oriented classroom is to help students learn and understand some important words and concepts related to thinking.

What Mary Did

We will begin by looking at how Mary introduced the vocabulary of thinking in the classroom. Mary began by asking her first graders to sit in a circle on the floor so that they might see and hear one another easily. She herself sat on a small chair. This is how she introduced the term *strategies* to her class:

> **Teacher (T):** *Who knows what a strategy is? Anybody knows what the word* strategy *means?*
> [Since the class remained silent, Mary stood up and wrote the word *strategy* on the board. She continued by asking:]
>
> **T:** *Anybody knows?*
>
> **Peter:** *Something you use to win a race.*
>
> **T:** *Something you use to win a race. What do you mean?*

Perhaps you have noticed that Mary introduced the word *strategy* by assessing her students' prior knowledge of the new term. This brief assessment would help her to adjust instruction to her students' needs.

Notice also that Mary repeated what Peter said, probably to make sure she was understanding him. Paraphrasing or repeating what has been said not only helped Mary clarify what Peter said; it also let Peter know that Mary was listening to him and had heard him. In that way it encouraged a positive relationship between them. Use paraphrasing with caution, however, since this technique may discourage students from listening to each other. When a teacher frequently speaks, even if repeating or rewording what students say, then children may learn to focus on the teacher's voice instead of valuing their own.

Mary used the open-ended question, "What do you mean?" to press Peter to elaborate on the definition he had given. Open-ended questions help to elicit children's thinking. Such questioning is an important feature of the flexible interview.

The discussion of the term *strategies* continued:

> **Peter:** *Something you use, to . . . say . . . solve math problems.*
> [At this point, Mary addressed the following question to the entire class:]
>
> **T:** *O.K., but what is it really? What does a strategy mean?*
>
> **John:** *You have to do something to find out a mystery.*
>
> **T:** *Is it a way to solve a mystery or to solve a problem?*

Despite Mary's good question, Peter had great difficulty saying what he was thinking about the term *strategies*. Notice how Mary accepted what he said and relieved him of further pressure by trying to involve the rest of the class.

Mary, connecting Peter's and John's definitions, suggested that a strategy is a "way" to solve either a mystery or a problem. Here Mary was helping her students construct a definition for the term *strategies*. When the teacher uses students' definitions to construct a working definition for the class, the word becomes more meaningful to the students. When children work together to construct the meaning of a word, they tend to relate to it personally, in the context of situations that are familiar to them. Often, vocabulary is taught in isolation, with very limited immediate, meaningful application. When words are taught in context, children are more likely to learn, use, and retain the new words for a long period of time.

Mary continued working on the term *strategies* by involving other students. Next, Ann raised her hand.

> **Ann:** *Another explanation of a strategy is, when you are in a race and you say: I need a strategy to help me, and you think of one. It is like you are planning a way to win a race, like you are planning a way to work.*
>
> **T:** *O.K. You are planning a way to work.*
> [At this point, while the dialogues were being conducted, John, a student in the classroom, stood up and began to wander.]
> **T:** *John, why don't you go back to where you were?*

Mary noticed immediately that John had begun to wander. With only a brief interruption in the flow of the discussion, she managed to urge him to return to his place in the circle. He was soon part of the group once more, and the discussion continued:

> **T:** *O.K., so it is a plan. A strategy is a plan or a way to figure something out. O.K.?*

We see that the last thing Mary did was to summarize what had been said about the term *strategies*. She presented a working definition that the class could relate to. It is very important to conclude and summarize thoughts after children have been discussing their thinking. This wraps up the discussion and provides some closure for students.

Mary used summarizing for another important purpose, too. As she and her students reached a consensus about the meaning of the word *strategy*, Mary used paraphrasing and summarizing to guide that consensus toward a useful and appropriate definition. She wanted her children to learn to think imaginatively, but she also wanted them to learn the conventional meanings of words. Beginning by accepting and validating her students' words, she then helped them to examine, compare, and refine their original beliefs. Finally her students were ready to use a shared vocabulary to discuss key aspects of their thinking.

What You Can Do

The right seating arrangement can facilitate a good discussion. In a circle or a semicircle, children can see and listen to one another. If students sit on the floor, you may want to sit on the floor with them, or you may prefer to find a small chair for yourself. Sitting at the same level as your students helps them to feel that you are a part of their team. It contributes to that accepting environment that is so important for the expression of thinking.

Perhaps you may wish to explain the purpose of your lesson more explicitly than Mary did. You may begin, for example, by telling your students that you will be solving mathematics problems together, but that this time you are not interested only in their answers. Rather, you would like them to talk about what they are thinking as they solve the problems. To start a discussion among your students about the communication of their thinking, you might ask, "Why is it important for us to learn about each other's thinking when we are solving a problem? What can we learn from listening to each other's thoughts?"

To introduce the need for vocabulary, ask, " What do you need if you want to talk about something?" Get students to see that it is easier to talk or write about a topic when we know something about it and when we have the right words to use. Help them to see that words help them to understand each other. Your students will be more interested in learning a new word if they believe that it will help them share their ideas. For instance, tell your students that they will learn to use a new word, *strategy*, in order to talk about their thinking.

We saw that Mary began her lesson with an informal assessment of her students' prior knowledge of the term *strategy*. You might wish to brainstorm with your students about the kinds of terms they would need to use in order to talk about their thinking. Some students may be unfamiliar with those terms. Others may not agree on their definitions. Help your students to see how important it may be to discuss those terms together in order to reach a common understanding of their meanings.

The ability to lead a discussion that will foster thinking in your classroom develops gradually, with practice. You will be off to a good start if you use three important techniques that Mary used: open-ended questioning, reflecting what students say, and summarizing as the discussion proceeds.

Open-ended questions encourage students to think aloud. An open-ended question does not suggest a particular answer. It requires the student to consider his or her own thought process. In answering, the student shares that thought process with the class. "Why did you say that?" or "How did you do it?" are two of the open-ended questions that Mary used.

Because they result in many different productive answers, open-ended questions also encourage other members of the discussion to think about how they would answer the question and to prepare to share their answers. When you ask, "What strategy did you use?" give your students enough time for many of them to be ready to offer an answer. Then you will be able to call on several students to share their strategies. If you don't give students enough time to think, only the fastest will have an answer. The slower students soon will learn from experience that it does not pay to think about an answer because they won't get called on anyway.

Like many other good discussion leaders, Mary paraphrased and repeated what her students said during the discussion. You, too, can act as a mirror, reflecting back to your class what they say. When you reflect their thoughts back to them, you show your students that you have heard them. You give them a chance to correct you when you have misunderstood them. You enable other class members to hear again their peers' valuable thoughts and to concentrate on the flow of ideas. In these ways, reflecting facilitates sharing of ideas. Reflecting can be visual, too. You will help the more visual learners in your class if you write an ongoing outline of the discussion on the board or with colored marker pens on a large sheet of paper.

Summarizing at the end of a discussion is an extension of paraphrasing and reflecting. Summarizing helps students review and integrate the results of the discussion. It allows you to point out to the class what they have accomplished. It gives you an opportunity to show your students how many of them have contributed to the development of a consensus or agreement as their ideas developed collaboratively.

Taken together, open-ended questioning, reflecting, and summarizing will help you to lead a productive discussion with ideas which come directly from your students. Your role is that of guide, facilitator, and coach.

Now let's look at the discussion from the point of the individual child. What kind of environment does each child need in order to be willing to share the ideas on which an exciting discussion about thinking can be built?

We saw how Mary listened, questioned, and coached students in order to encourage them to say what they were thinking. Above all, Mary showed respect for her students' thinking. She valued what each one of them had to say. There is no question that such an approach has an impact on the atmosphere in the classroom.

If you wish students to talk about their thinking, you will wish to establish in your classroom the kind of risk-free environment in which children trust you and trust each other. Often, a student who is a good thinker will fail to get the right answer even though he or she has a very reasonable strategy. The strategy may be valuable even if the answer is not correct. But if your students are not sure that they have the right answer, they may not offer to share unless they know that their ideas will be respected whether their answer is complete or incomplete, right or wrong.

We saw how Mary tried to involve several students in the discussion. It is important to involve all of your students, little by little, in talking about their thinking. The major concern of the teachers we worked with was getting everyone in the class to talk. These teachers were surprised to see that when they worked with flexible interviewing in the classroom, most, if not all, of their students became involved in the communication of thinking. Even shy students became capable of talking about their thoughts.

In Mary's example, we also saw how her quick intervention prevented one child's wandering from becoming a disrupting influence. Although Mary was successful in getting John to sit down, you might think of more direct ways to accomplish that. If the teacher asks, "Would you like to . . . ?" or "Why don't you . . . ?" the student may answer in a negative way. It may be less risky to make a simple request: "John, please sit down."

Unobtrusive management of distractions and interruptions is a very important aspect of the environment of the thinking classroom. Even in the most democratic environments, there are situations in which certain behaviors are expected in order for the work to get done. A democracy would not work otherwise. It is most important that students know ahead of time what is expected of them. Rules, limits, logical consequences, and self-discipline need to be established at the outset in every classroom. Children function best in structured environments in which they are held responsible for behaving as expected. Clear limits, consistently maintained, eliminate most disruptions and permit concentration on thinking and learning.

Once you have begun to make your classroom into a place where thinking is the focus of the curriculum, you may find new rewards in teaching. Try it yourself and you will see! Let us know about your experience.

Here are some guidelines that may help you as you introduce the vocabulary of thinking into your own classroom.

1. Arrange the seating to foster communication.
2. Communicate to your students the purpose of the lesson.
3. Motivate your students to use the language of thinking.
4. Assess your students' knowledge of each term.
5. Teach each vocabulary term in context.
6. Guide your students to construct their own meanings of the term.
7. Accept the informal wordings in which your students express their thoughts.
8. Use open-ended questions.
9. Listen carefully and teach your students to be good listeners.
10. Paraphrase or reflect your students' thoughts.
11. Do not pressure your students to talk.
12. Accept and value your students' thinking.
13. Let your students know that learning to talk about thinking is not easy.
14. Use positive, straightforward management techniques.
15. Summarize the discussion with your students.

▲ Learning to Plan and to Talk about What One Is Going to Do

Planning is an important part of problem solving. Once children feel comfortable with the vocabulary of thinking, you can begin to teach them how to plan their work and how to talk about their plans.

Several different goals are accomplished when children learn to plan together. Children know better what is expected of them. They are better prepared to work independently and effectively. They learn how to think and to control their thoughts and actions. They become less likely to rush to compute before they know which computations will help solve the problem.

When they plan together, students learn also that there are alternative approaches to solving a problem; there is not just one right way. An emphasis on planning helps shift the focus of the lesson from getting the answer to finding a strategy to figure out the problem. Planning together encourages thinking; in order to talk about their thinking, children need to reflect upon their thoughts.

In our experimental work, teachers found it beneficial to work with their students in several areas:

- Developing the ability to think before engaging in problem solving
- Developing the ability to discuss their plans with others
- Developing the ability to listen to one another's thoughts

What Mary Did

We have seen how Mary introduced the vocabulary of thinking and motivated her students to engage in reflecting on the thinking process. Next, she gave her students an opportunity to apply within a familiar context what they had learned about strategies. She gave them a word problem to solve.

Mary brought to class the following word problem written on a large piece of paper:

A man had a bicycle shop. In his shop he had 15 wheels. How many bicycles did he have? How many tricycles did he have?

The first thing Mary did was to ask her students to read the problem silently. Then she answered children's questions about the problem. Mary wanted to be sure that her students developed a good understanding of the problem. Understanding the problem is a very important step in the problem-solving process. Giving students enough time to read, think, and understand the task they are about to engage in saves time in the long run.

Now let's look at how Mary asked her students to plan and to talk about the plans they would use to solve the word problem.

> *T: Before you go off to solve these problems, raise your hands and tell me if you . . . don't give me your answers. I don't even want the answer right now, if you think you know it. I want to know some ways that . . . some ways that you think you could figure this problem out. Some strategies you might use to figure this problem out.*

Note that Mary is asking her students to talk about their plans in terms of strategies that could be used to solve a problem. As you may recall, *strategies* was the new vocabulary term introduced during Mary's previous lesson. Now Mary is relating what has been learned recently to a new situation. Immediate application of the vocabulary learned provides the context for meaningful learning. The context reinforces the learning of the new word. At the same time, the new word enhances the students' planning skills as they work together on a problem.

This is how Mary's students shared their strategies:

> *Erika: You could count by 2's.*
> *T: Why would you do that?*

At this point, Mary asked an open-ended question: "Why would you do that?" This is the kind of question that presses students to think and to talk about their thinking. Open-ended questions teach students skills, such as planning skills. At the same time, they teach students how to think.

> *Erika: Well, because . . . say there were 6 wheels in the store, and the store only had bicycles . . . that would mean you had 3 bicycles.*

As she had done in the previous lesson, Mary wrote students' strategies on the board or on a large sheet of paper. A visual record may help students learn from each other.

> *T: Erika would count by two's. Is that what you said, Erika?*
> *Erika: Yeah.*

> *T: Who else has another idea about what strategy they would use to solve this problem?*
>
> **Derrick:** *You could take a piece of paper and put 15 dots and then you could draw a dot for a wheel and you would end up with the answer.*
>
> *T: Great! So, you would use paper and pencil and you would draw dots on your paper to represent each wheel. And then you would try to figure out from that how many bicycles and tricycles there were? Is that your strategy?*
>
> **Derrick:** *Yes.*

Mary drew another student into the discussion. We see that, as she had done before, Mary paraphrased what her students said. In this example, we also see how Mary provided immediate feedback to her students. Children benefit from positive feedback when they are doing a good job. They need to know that the teacher is aware of the effort they are making. This will increase their motivation to work and make them feel more secure as learners.

> *T: Good. Any other strategy?*
>
> **Douglas:** *I have a strategy. You could, ah . . . you could, ah . . . draw circles on a paper, and then put 2 of whatever you are using on a paper, and then 2 wheels would equal a bike and 3 wheels would equal a tricycle.*
>
> *T: So, you would use paper and pencil and pictures, right? Great!*

Notice how Mary listened and gave Douglas time to express his idea. This is a very important aspect of the thinking classroom. Children need to feel that the teacher values their thoughts enough to allow sufficient time for them to communicate those thoughts.

Now let us take a look at the strategies Mary's students suggested. Here are three of the strategies Mary recorded:

- Erika would count by 2's.
- Derrick would draw dots and count them.
- Douglas would draw 2 circles to represent a bicycle and 3 circles to represent a tricycle.

Erika suggested a counting strategy. She also appeared to know that this bicycle-and-tricycle problem is a particular case of a more general problem. She used as an example a different particular case involving only 6 wheels and only bicycles. Then she used that simpler problem as a starting point for solving the 15-wheel problem. Her practice of solving a simpler related problem first in order to solve a more difficult problem is a very productive strategy, indeed.

Derrick suggested modeling the problem on paper, using a dot to represent each wheel. He said that he would use those dots to solve the problem. He did not say how he would do this, but it is likely that he would have succeeded. He might have used Erika's counting strategy in some way. Modeling a problem is another excellent problem-solving strategy.

Douglas suggested drawing circles to represent the wheels. His strategy built on those suggested by his classmates. He used a counting strategy that involved grouping by 2 and by 3. He carried Derrick's modeling strategy one step further by specifying the need to use 2 wheels for a bicycle and 3 wheels for a tricycle. Moreover, he showed that he knows that either a dot or a circle may represent a wheel. It does not matter which symbol is chosen to represent the real object in the problem. When he says, "or whatever you are using," he is thinking very abstractly. It shows that Douglas is quite conscious of the arbitrary nature of the symbols that may be used to represent the wheels described in the problem.

Notice that each child's strategy was different. Taken together, they provide a rich set of complementary strategies. Each child appears to have heard the others. Each strategy builds in some way on the ones that came before. Each child can evaluate and modify his or her own strategy during such a sharing process. Mary's questioning truly leads her students to think.

Students who may not know at first how to share their strategies may learn by listening to their peers and using their plans as models. Later, they will learn how to get started on their own. Students who have an inefficient way of solving a problem may begin to think about it in a different way. Students also will learn to accept that there may be alternative approaches to solving a problem.

What You Can Do

When you begin to invite your students to share their problem-solving strategies, you will find that you want to use a problem that is not so simple that the answer is obvious. Many good problems, like Mary's wheel problem, have more than one correct answer. In Mary's problem, some information must be supplied by the student. The student must know that a bicycle has 2 wheels and a tricycle has 3. That information is not given in the problem statement. Mary's students also had to make assumptions about how to interpret the problem. For example, they assumed that all the wheels would be used. A good problem, then, is not too simple; it may have more than one right answer; it may require some additional information to be supplied from the students' knowledge of the real world; it may need to be more precisely defined by the students; and it probably can be solved in a variety of different ways. Such a problem is capable of supporting an interesting discussion.

Because interesting problems are not simple, it is especially important that all students understand the problem before sharing their strategies for solving it. After you and your students read the problem, you will want to make sure that your students have enough time to ask questions to clarify any uncertainties that they might have. When a problem needs further definition, your students can decide together what assumptions should be made. Interesting real-world problems like the wheel problem often are not tidy when they first appear. If a problem is too simple, students are apt to skip over the important process of understanding and clarifying it.

A focus on learning how to plan helps shift students' attention away from just getting an answer. A thinking-oriented classroom is concerned with the thinking processes underlying the end result. Once your students read and understand a problem, it is appropriate to let them know that you would like them to discuss their strategies before they produce their answers. It may be difficult for them to understand that you would like them to depart from the more usual way of solving a problem. Probably they will want to solve it quickly and give you the answer. Thus, you must be ready to deal with this issue directly and convince them of the importance of planning. Using open-ended questions and paraphrasing or reflecting students' replies help you to keep the discussion focused on process rather than product.

In the thinking-oriented classroom, in which students share their thoughts about the meanings of words and about problem-solving strategies, much time is spent sharing. You may ask, "If I spend all that time with my students in discussion, how will I ever cover all the math that I am obliged to cover?" In fact, you may not be able to solve as many problems with your students. You may spend more time on each of a much smaller number of problems.

But if you really want to teach students to think about math instead of just doing math mechanically, then "Less is more" must be your motto. Let us look at some issues relating to the use of time in your thinking classroom.

When you are beginning to develop a thinking classroom, will the class be ready to listen patiently and wait for a student to express his or her ideas? You may need to discuss this issue openly with your students, highlighting the importance of listening to their peers' thoughts.

In timing discussions, it is all a matter of getting the right balance. You need to be sensitive to how much time your class is ready to give to listening to others. You are the only one who can make this decision because you are the one who knows the group well. Try little by little to make the group sensitive to one another's needs and supportive of their peers. Model for them how to listen, accept, and value what others have to say. Such a caring environment will allow your students to develop their thinking skills as they grow in acquiring security and strong self-esteem as learners.

Despite students' positive attitudes toward listening to others, some of them will sometimes take too long to talk. You may have to stop one student in order to give another child an opportunity to talk and to maintain a positive atmosphere in the class. If you have to stop a child, be sure to give him or her a chance to express the ideas either at another time or in another way. You might say, for example: "Take your time and think about it. When you are ready to talk, raise your hand and let us all know what you are thinking. We all are interested in what you have to contribute." Or: "Write down your ideas and give them to me (or read them to us) at the end of the class. We are eager to know what you are thinking."

Anticipating or planning what one is going to do is not easy. When children begin to learn how to talk about their thinking, they need to be given time to do so. It takes time and practice to put one's thoughts together and express them coherently. Children need to be encouraged to work at it. When the teacher points to students' growth at each step of the process, they generally cope better with the difficulties inherent in the task.

Mary asked her students to talk about their plans, but there may be other ways in which you may wish to accomplish the same goal in your class. For example, you may want to ask your students to write their plans, draw them, record them on audio or videotape, or talk to their peers about them.

To review, in order to teach your students how to plan and how to talk about their plans, follow these steps:

1. Arrange the seating to foster communication.
2. Tell your students that the lesson is about planning.
3. Motivate your students to think about what they will be doing.
4. Present an interesting problem.
5. Give your students time to read and understand the problem.
6. Give your students time to think and plan.
7. Ask your students to communicate their plans (it could be through talking, writing, or drawing).
8. Discuss with your class the importance of listening to their peers' plans.
9. Give your students time to communicate their plans to each other.
10. Question your students' plans (preferably using open-ended questions).
11. Paraphrase your students' ideas.
12. Give immediate feedback.

▲ Learning to Record One's Thinking

Once children begin to feel comfortable talking about their plans, you can teach them how to record their work in writing. Generally, children do not write about their thinking. In many classrooms, however, writing and math are being linked through journals, logs, and other writing procedures.

Learning to write about one's thinking is very useful. Writing helps develop mathematics skills, thinking skills, and communication skills as well. When students record their thinking they are learning how to think about math, to write about math, and to share their ideas with others.

Writing is useful not only for students; it also helps the teacher assess how well students express their thinking and what strategies they employ. If we want to assess students' work in a thinking-oriented classroom, we should help students learn to express their thinking not just orally, but also in writing.

Our experience in classrooms shows that teachers found it beneficial to work with students in developing the ability to record their thinking using different methods, including the following:

- Written text
- Pictures
- Mathematical symbols
- Number sentences
- Equations

What Mary Did

Mary began by asking her students to work independently to solve the bicycle-and-tricycle word problem. She also asked them to write down the strategies they had used to solve it. Let's see how Mary explained to her students how to record their strategies.

Mary herself modeled for her students how she recorded her own thinking. Modeling is a good way to explain how to do something unfamiliar, because it lets students see and hear a concrete example.

> **T:** *After you have figured out your answer, I want you to write it down on this piece of paper (shows). Let's say I've used Unifix cubes and I figured it out. Right, I got my answer. What I would do then, is I would draw the Unifix cubes, how I arranged them, and underneath them I would write my strategy. I would say, "I used Unifix cubes. I made each Unifix cube represent one wheel," or whatever it is that you did.*

As Mary modeled writing and thinking aloud, she gave students an idea of how to get started. Note that Mary did not give students specific, step-by-step instructions for how to record their thinking. Instead, she left the task quite open. She was careful to suggest that students might have strategies that were different from hers. She said, "Let's say I've used Unifix cubes . . . or whatever it is that you did."

Once Mary had given her explanation, students solved the problems and wrote down their strategies. Let's take a look at how they recorded those strategies. The records we are about to see were the result of their first experience in writing down what they had done.

As you read about Mary's students, notice the kind of information that students are able to externalize through their records. Think about what conclusions you can draw about the students' thinking from their written records.

First, let's see what Jenny recorded as her strategy:

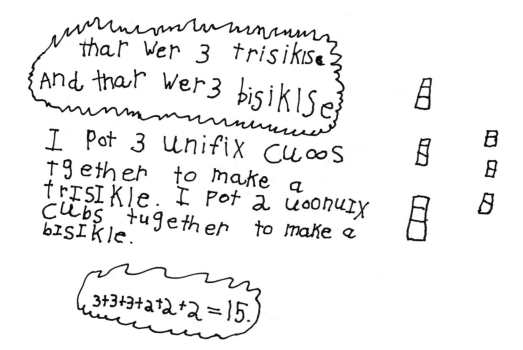

that wer 3 trisikis.
And that wer 3 bisikIse

I Pot 3 unifix cuoos tgether to make a trISIKle. I Pot 2 uoonuIx cubs tugether to make a bISIKle.

$$3+3+3+2+2+2 = 15.$$

Jenny wrote, "There were 3 tricycles and there were 3 bicycles. I put 3 Unifix cubes together to make a tricycle. I put 2 Unifix cubes together to make a bicycle." Jenny also drew the cubes.

From Jenny's record we can tell several things. It is clear that she used Unifix cubes to solve the problem successfully. We also know that she used one cube to represent each wheel. In her written words she gave her answer and she explained that she used Unifix cubes to represent wheels, 3 for a tricycle and 2 for a bicycle. Her pictures give more information. They show how she arranged the groups.

Still, we are unable to tell what strategy she used to determine that she had used exactly 15 wheels. She may have counted the wheels one by one as she was drawing and grouping. Or she may have counted by 2's or by 3's. She may have drawn each cube as she counted it. Or she may have drawn 15 cubes first and then grouped them by 2 or by 3. It is important to know which strategy was used, since each strategy reflects a different level of mathematical thinking. For example, counting one by one reflects a less advanced thinking strategy than counting by 2's or by 3's.

Often it is useful to conduct mini-interviews about written records. Mary might have discovered Jenny's counting strategy if she had asked, "Could you show us how you counted?"

Next, let's take a look at what Cory wrote as his strategy:

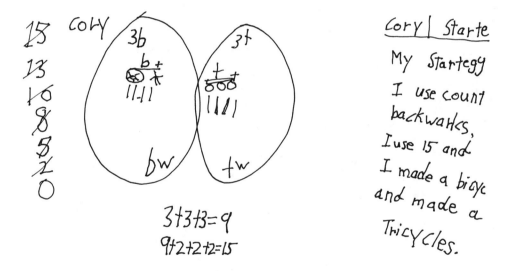

Cory wrote, "My strategy I use count backwards. I use 15 and I made a bicycle and made a tricycle."

The information we can get from Cory's record shows how he used two strategies. It is clear from his picture that he arranged groups of 2 and 3, but from his pictures we do not know how he actually arrived at his answer. The information he may have gotten from counting backwards was not explicitly reported. Here, again, Mary might ask a question such as, "Could you explain your picture to us?"

Here is Ellen's strategy:

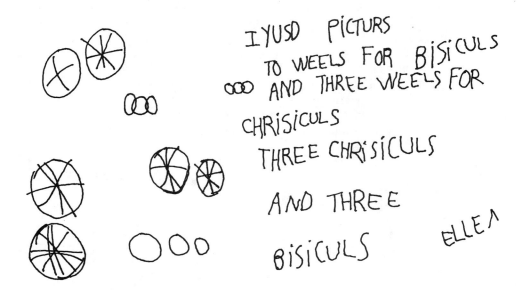

$$2 + 2 + 2 + 3 + 3 + 3 = 15$$

I YUSD PICTURS TO WEELS FOR BISICULS AND THREE WEELS FOR CHRISICULS THREE CHRISICULS AND THREE BISICULS

ELLEN

Ellen wrote: "I used pictures. Two wheels for bicycles and 3 wheels for tricycles. Three tricycles and 3 bicycles." Her drawings showed groups of two and three wheels.

From Ellen's record, we can tell several things. It is clear that she used her own pictures, rather than manipulatives. Two wheels represent a bicycle and 3 wheels represent a tricycle. Her pictures actually represent the numbers she included in her number sentence.

Again, what is missing from Ellen's record is the strategy. We do not know what she thought as she solved the problem. A mini-interview would help explore her thinking further.

What conclusions can we draw about these students' thinking by looking at their written records? The students' written narration of their thinking may not have been full enough to give us an understanding of what they did. Their drawings certainly complement what they wrote. What is missing from all the records is the strategy. We do not know how they figured out the problem. How did they decide whether to use Unifix cubes or pictures? How did they know when they had used exactly 15 wheels? Did they count by 1's, by 2's, or by 3's? Did they add mentally? Did they add using pencil and paper? These are important aspects of students' thinking, which are definitely not clear from their records. But written records provide concrete evidence of students' thinking and a good basis for further questioning in a mini-interview. One teacher proposed that when verbal questioning alone is not productive, pictures can provide access to student thinking. She said: "With the children who are having difficulty . . . I have them draw pictures to show what they're thinking. And then they can explain it."

If you ask your students to explain what they have written you often can get a very good assessment of their mathematical thinking.

What You Can Do

After your students have solved a problem using cubes, blocks, or pictures, how will you get them started at recording their strategies? Students often learn more easily when you give them a model to follow. At first, they may imitate you. Mary's students imitated her use of Unifix cubes. With practice, however, they may begin to approach the task in their own ways.

Mary was careful to model general guidelines about how to record her work, without giving her students a detailed or complete routine to follow. If, like Mary, you indicate a general method without giving too much detail, you will encourage your students to be creative and resourceful.

At first your students may produce very simple written records similar to those we have just seen. Elementary school students need your coaching, practice, and feedback to be able to come up with records that explain fully what they were thinking and what they did.

To broaden the information students provide you with, you can always follow up the written records with a mini–flexible interview. You can ask open-ended questions, such as these:

"How did you figure out that there were 3 bicycles and 3 tricycles?"

"Why did you use Unifix cubes?"

"Did using Unifix cubes help you?"

"What did you do to determine that you had already used all 15 wheels?"

Tailor your questions to elicit whatever information is not shown in the students' words and pictures.

Ask students to read out loud what they have written. This will help them think, reflect, listen to themselves, and identify ideas that may be incomplete.

Going through the experience of the interview will help students develop further their ability to think, reflect, and express their thinking. As students learn to value the importance of the additional information that you question them about, they will be encouraged to include the same kinds of information in their future written records.

There are useful ways to extend Mary's work in your classroom. In addition to asking your students to record what they did when they solved a problem, you can ask other questions:

"What did you learn while you were solving this problem?"

"What makes you a good problem solver?"

"Do you like solving problems?"

"Is this problem hard or easy? Why do you say that?"

"What did you learn from someone else about this problem?"

If you ask your students to keep math journals or portfolios of their work, you will be able to use these for assessment purposes. Equally important, students will be able to use them to assess their own learning.

When you review your students' records, you will be able to judge what kind of instruction is most beneficial for a particular student. You will learn how much an individual student's thinking has developed. You can also gauge a student's progress in learning how to write about his or her thinking. Last, but certainly not least, you will be able to show students' writing to parents to support your remarks during a parent conference. Thus, records are important assessment and teaching tools, not only at the point in time at which they are produced, but later on as well.

Self-evaluation helps students to develop an awareness of their strengths and weaknesses. When students have helped to define their own needs, they are better prepared to set appropriate learning goals for themselves. You can ask students to assess their own progress in math and in writing about math by asking,

"How do you think you are doing in math?"

"What do you like (or dislike) most about math?"

"What do you do best in math?"

"What is hardest for you?"

"Why do you think this is hard for you?"

"What do you need more help with?"

"Is it easy for you to write about your strategy? Why?"

If you do want to use students' written records for assessment and self-assessment in your classroom, here are some ways that our teachers have used to collect students' work.

The use of the word processor in writing about mathematics is a phenomenal way to develop students' motivation to write while also fostering their thinking. You can ask your students to keep a writing folder in the computer and to record their thinking whenever they carry out a mathematics activity.

In language arts, portfolios have become a popular way of keeping records of students' writing progress. Similar kinds of records can be kept in mathematics. You can ask your students to create their own pocket folders by drawing on two pieces of cardboard and putting them together. They can then begin to keep all of their math writing work in these folders. Writing about mathematics can become a part of their language arts work.

A math notebook is another simple way to keep a record of students' writing. The benefit of having a notebook is that records are less likely to get lost. If it is in a notebook that can be taken home, parents can probably also take a look at their children's work and progress more often than if it is in a folder that must be kept at school.

The class as a whole may "publish" books about how they solved a problem. Although one student may design the cover, such a book belongs to the whole class. Each student has contributed a page. When the book contains a variety of ways that different students have solved a problem, it is a concrete reminder that problems can be solved in different ways, that different strategies may be successful, and that different strategies are valued by the class.

In any event, there are many ways to keep a record of students' writing. You may consider each of them and decide on which is best for your class.

To review, in order to teach your students how to record their thinking, here are some guidelines to follow:

1. Present a word problem involving a familiar context.
2. Model your own way of recording your thinking, by writing and by thinking aloud as you write.
3. Ask your students to record their own strategies in any way they wish.
4. Coach your students as they record their strategies.
5. Question your students about what they are writing, using open-ended questions.
6. Ask your students to read their records out loud.
7. Paraphrase your students' records.
8. Ask your students to evaluate their records for completeness.
9. Question your students to get more information about their strategies, feelings, and thoughts.
10. Use word processors, portfolios, folders, notebooks, or classroom publishing to collect and preserve students' writing.

▲ *Learning to Talk about What One Has Done*

We have seen how children can learn to talk about what they will do—that is, about their plans—and how they can write about what they have done. But we have noted that young children's written records usually do not explain their strategies completely. We saw that it often is useful for the teacher to question students about their written records in order to get more information.

Talking about what one has done is not the same as talking about planning. Different sets of skills are needed. As we have said before, planning requires the ability to manipulate certain information mentally, to anticipate and abstract what may happen. On the other hand, talking about what has been done demands that we reflect and think about the process we have carried out. Without training and practice, it is not easy for children to engage either in talking about planning or in talking about what has been done.

One teacher's observations illustrate the difference that training and practice can make. She says:

> I think it makes a great deal of difference how easily children are able to speak about their thoughts. After having a multi-age group, when you have the kids for two years, when you see them in the beginning they're kind of reserved and shy, and they're not quite sure whether this is the right thing to say, or maybe this is not acceptable, or maybe I'm way off base. My seconds this year are much more open, much more outgoing, much more able to say, "Hey, this is the way that I do it." I see a great deal of growth in the way they talk and the way they write.

Why is learning to talk about one's thinking so difficult? First of all, the kind of reflection required in mathematics may be different from what we do when carrying out an everyday activity. Reflection in mathematics may require that we reconstruct a sequence of events in an orderly way. For example, to talk about how we solved a problem, we must reconstruct each step of the process we followed in the order in which we carried it out. It is a major language task to describe a sequence of events in proper order.

Sometimes reflection in mathematics may require the reconstruction of a set of relations—for example, that one square is larger than another one, or one boy is taller than another. Both involve putting complex thoughts into words. It is difficult for young children to express with simple words the relation between two or more objects or situations. Learning to use correctly words such as *if, more, less, before, after, between, greater than, same as,* and *equal to* requires much time and experience.

In addition to ideas of order and relations, mathematics concepts such as *equivalence* and *commutativity* must themselves be well understood if they are to be put into words that someone else can understand. A young child may use the term *equals* without understanding the concept of equivalence. Because they know that $2 + 2 = 4$, children commonly think that *equals* means that the answer is coming up.

The language of mathematics is a demanding one, but it is worth learning. Several goals are accomplished when children learn to talk about their thinking. First, the language of mathematics helps children to plan, to reflect on what they have done, and to put their thinking into words. As they listen to one another, children use that language to share their thoughts and to learn from one another.

What Mary Did

We will continue to look at how Mary taught her students to talk in front of the group about their thinking. Mary began by asking her students open-ended questions. She attempted to elicit their thoughts about what went on when they solved the problem.

Gail: I used a dotted line and I discovered that . . . there were . . . that, I got 3 bicycles and 3 tricycles, but then I counted by 3's and I got all of them tricycles, so I got both answers.

T: O.K., so you got two answers. Show everybody what you did. [Student shows paper.] *Now, what do you mean by the dotted line? What did each dot represent in your strategy?*

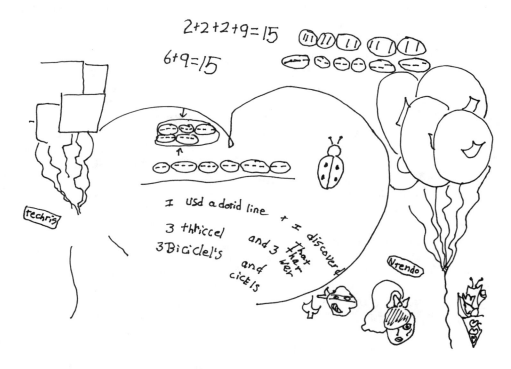

Notice that Mary paraphrased what Gail said. Mary used an open-ended question—"What do you mean by the dotted line?"— followed by a more specific one—"What did each dot represent in your strategy?" As we will see, an open-ended question was not explicit enough by itself to get Gail to explain her thinking.

Gail: A tricycle and a bicycle.

T: What did each dot represent? A tricycle or a bicycle?

Gail: A tricycle or a bicycle.

T: How come you drew 15 tricycles? What was each dot? You drew 15 dots. Why 15 dots? What was each dot?

Gail: Each dot was . . .

At this point in the interview, it is obvious that Gail is confused. Mary had asked several questions, one after the other. It is better not to ask too many questions at once. Gail might have felt more comfortable if Mary had asked questions one by one and had given her time to think and to respond.

Ethel: A wheel.

T: What did you say, Ethel?

Ethel: A wheel.

T: A wheel, and then you circled them, right? So you would circle . . . how many did you circle to make a bike?

Gail: [Pointing at drawing] A bicycle and a tricycle, a bicycle and a tricycle.

Ethel's intervention was helpful. It took the pressure off Gail, who was having a hard time thinking and responding to the teacher's questions. Once Gail's report was clarified, Mary continued asking her students to talk about their thinking. As usual, Mary tried to involve the rest of the class in the discussion.

When Mary's students were writing, it was hard for them to communicate the strategy they had used. The same was true when they tried to share their thinking out loud. For instance, in this last example we saw Gail struggling to indicate what each dot represented and how she had decided to group them to form bicycles or tricycles.

Let's see how Mary coached Stephanie, who had even greater difficulty expressing her strategy.

T: Stephanie, what did you do?
   [Stephanie does not respond.]

T: What did you use?
   [Stephanie does not respond.]

T: Those wooden cubes?
   [Stephanie nods her head, confirming what the teacher said.]

Like Stephanie, some children need to be coached more than others in order to communicate their thinking. By asking a series of questions that give more and more specific cues, you can provide that support. It is important, however, not to put words into children's mouths. For example, Mary's question ("What did you use?") is good in that it does not provide any specific information. Then Mary continued by asking Stephanie a very specific question, "Those wooden cubes?" Stephanie answered that she did use these blocks, and yet she may not actually have done so. Perhaps Mary had seen Stephanie use the cubes and wanted to help Stephanie get started with her explanation. It is difficult for us to tell whether she actually did use the cubes or whether she nodded yes just to please her teacher.

Let's take a look at how Stephanie had recorded her strategy:

Stephanie: *I noticed there were 3 of each, 3 tricycles and 3 bicycles.*
T: *Very good, Stephanie, very nicely done.*

Did Stephanie tell her teacher how she figured out there were 3 bicycles and 3 tricycles? No. There is no way to figure out Stephanie's strategy from her verbal report, although her written record helps clarify some of what she did. The next student questioned, Donald, was far more articulate.

T: *Now, Donald.*

Donald: *I used keys. I got the same answer as Max did, 6 bikes and 1 tricycle, and I did it this way: I circled every 2 [shows paper] keys and then I had 3, so that, I called a tricycle so I got 1 tricycle and 6 bicycles.*

This is Donald's work:

As we can see in this last example, it is easier for some children than for others to express their thinking. Some need more teacher support than others to talk about their strategies. Notice that a facility with words is not always accompanied by accuracy in computation. You will find that some students are very good at sharing an incorrect solution to a problem.

What You Can Do

It takes time for children to learn how to express their thoughts in a way that makes sense to others. Your questions can help your students learn how to express their thoughts clearly. There are individual differences in how much support children need in order to verbalize their thinking.

Open-ended questions are best for beginning to question a student. They give the least support and demand the most from the student. They also give the student the greatest opportunity for free expression of his or her thoughts. When the student needs more help, a more specific question will serve as a cue to elicit a particular answer. As an interviewer you will want to find a balance between open-ended and more specific questions. The degree of specificity or cueing that your question provides will depend on how much support you think the student needs. Only you will know how specific to be in order to get children to express their thinking.

The children who need the most support and coaching to learn to talk about their thinking are the ones who require the most specific questions or cues. Children who have learned how to talk about their thinking will be cued to do so with only a few open-ended questions. The task for the interviewer is to get the less experienced students to learn to talk about their thinking. Cues provided in specific questions will, in the long run, teach children what kinds of information they should be aware of when they are asked to report on their work. Over time, they will learn to give fuller responses with fewer cues.

Don't feel frustrated if you find that your students are unable to describe completely the strategy they have used. With time and practice, the majority of them will increasingly be able to do so.

On the basis of our general experience in the classroom, it appears that some children feel more comfortable talking about their thinking after they have first been given time to write about it. In fact, a beginning stage for many of them was to read what they had written. Little by little, they became comfortable enough to talk about their thinking, without having to read.

Teachers have to learn to question, just as students have to learn to respond. It is not easy to question children's thinking on the spot. Interviewers find themselves frequently revising the way they approach questioning. As a beginning interviewer you may find yourself talking too much, rather than questioning and listening. Or you may find yourself asking too many questions at once.

Although you may be able to plan in advance some of the questions you want to ask, you often will need to improvise. Some of the best questions are contingent on students' answers. It takes practice, time, and experience to become a good interviewer.

As you begin, here are some guidelines to help you teach your students to talk about what they have done.

1. Motivate your students to talk about what they have done.
2. Present a word problem involving a familiar context.
3. Ask your students to solve the problem and record their work.
4. Use open-ended questions to ask your students to explain their written work.
5. Determine whether an open-ended question or a more specific question is needed to elicit the information required.
6. Ask more specific questions to help your students clarify what they are saying.
7. Coach your students if necessary with cues and specific questions to help them express their thinking.
8. Avoid embarrassing a student who is unable to speak.
9. Try to give many students an opportunity to speak.

▲ Reflecting on the Experience of Learning

A very important goal in the thinking classroom is that students learn to be reflective about their own learning. We want them to evaluate their own learning experience. We want them to be able to think about what they are learning, the goals of learning, the learning experience, the uses of what they are learning, the implications of what they are learning, their strengths and weaknesses in learning a particular task, their effort, and their feelings toward learning.

It is useful to teach children how to reflect on their own learning for at least two reasons. First, students can begin to have a voice in the curriculum. For example, children can discuss their learning activities and propose changes in them. They can also suggest variations in the content of the curriculum to adjust it better to their interests and needs. In essence, reflection on the learning experience helps children become active learners. They become direct participants in the teaching–learning process. In addition, the teacher can use the information obtained from students' reflections to adjust instruction to their needs.

Several goals are accomplished when children learn how to reflect on their work. The reflection upon one's learning develops thinking. Students are motivated as they develop an awareness of their strengths, weaknesses, needs, interests, and so on. Students are more likely to work toward a goal if they are aware of how its achievement may favorably affect themselves as learners.

What Mary Did

One way to involve students in reflection is to engage them in the process of evaluating a learning experience. Let's look at how Mary conducted an activity in which she did just that. In her lesson, Mary engaged her students in the process of reflecting on their learning by asking the question, "Is it hard or easy?" After students talked about how they solved the bicycle problem, she asked them to write a number sentence to represent their solution. The next dialogues show how the children talked about what made this task "hard" or "easy":

> *T: I saw some people sharing. Tell me something, how was this today? Was this hard or easy?*
>
> *Class: Easy . . . Hard . . . Easy . . . Easy . . . Hard*
>
> *T: Let's hear from people who thought it was hard and from people who thought it was easy. Let's hear from both.*
>
> *Eric: Well, it was hard, because I did not know what to do with the number sentence.*
>
> *T: All right, so you found it hard, because you did not know what to do with the number sentence. That confused you.*
>
> *Corinne: I think it was really hard, because I couldn't figure out a number sentence.*
>
> *T: All right, so you had trouble figuring out the number sentence. So, look, two people found it hard. That's perfectly natural.*

At this point, notice how Mary accepts students' difficulties. She makes it clear that it is natural for some children to find it difficult to work on the task. This kind of nonjudgmental attitude toward students certainly provides relief for those who may not be able to carry out a task. It is a perfect example of the special kind of atmosphere that needs to be developed in order for children to talk about their thinking. For a student to admit openly that an activity is difficult, an accepting environment needs to be in place.

Let's continue to look at how Mary handled this discussion.

> **Erika:** *I found it kind of easy*
>
> **T:** *You found it easy. How come?*
>
> **Erika:** *Well, I just thought of my strategy, the one I did the first time and I kind of used it to solve the problem.*
>
> **T:** *You thought about the strategy that you used last week, and then you added to it?*

Notice how Mary paraphrases what Erika says. She is showing how well she listens, while also modeling this skill for her students. This is how Mary continues:

> **T:** *Can I ask everybody to put their sheet in front of them and not to rustle it? And move back, Harry, so you can let Stephanie in the circle. And we need David in the circle also. Come on David, move over here.*

Notice that the seating arrangement is an important element in the appropriate atmosphere for listening. Mary's students began to become inattentive when they were not fully included in the circle on the floor.

As we can see, Mary had to stop the class to handle the management problem. Notice how, this time, Mary used positive, direct statements to deal with the situation. She did not need to scream at the children, nor did she get angry. The situation was handled quickly and the class continued.

> **Stephanie:** *I thought it was kind of hard, at first, but when Becky helped me, I thought it was kind of easy.*
>
> **T:** *You know, I thought that was something very nice to happen. I was there first, helping Becky and she got it easily. And then, she helped Stephanie get it, right?*

Positive feedback such as Mary gives to her students is quite important. It helps students become aware of which kinds of behaviors are expected and encouraged in the classroom. Further, notice that the child who voluntarily talked about her difficulty is Stephanie.

Recall that Stephanie had much difficulty expressing her thinking in the previous lesson. The growth in her ability to communicate is surely related to the supportive environment in Mary's classroom.

> *T: Did you like helping Stephanie? Was it easy or hard?*
>
> **Becky:** *It wasn't really hard, because after I knew what to do, I just could help her.*
>
> *T: So, after you knew what to do, it was easier to help her.*

At this point, notice how spontaneous peer tutoring develops into collaborative learning. Becky became engaged in tutoring Stephanie and was successful at it. Not only did Stephanie develop an understanding of the activity, she also felt good about herself as a learner, because she was able to carry out the task. Their collaboration was facilitated by the risk-free classroom environment.

> **Erika:** *I thought it was easy, because the number sentence was really right in front of my face.*
>
> *T: The number sentence was right in front of your face. What do you mean by that? Oh, you mean the pictures were right in front of your face?*
>
> **Erika:** *Yeah, so the pictures were really the number sentence.*

As children listen to their peers talk about the effectiveness of the strategies they have used, they learn new approaches to problem solving. They have opportunities to evaluate each other's strategies as well as their own.

What You Can Do

Although it is not easy for children to engage in reflection, you can help them learn this skill. Leave a few minutes at the end of the lesson for students to discuss their feelings and thoughts about it.

To assess students' thoughts, vary the questions you ask, adjusting them to suit the activities of the lesson. For example, you may ask,

> "How do you feel when you talk about your thinking?"
>
> "How do you feel when you are unable to solve a problem?"
>
> "What did you learn from listening to your classmates?"

"After listening to each other's strategies, what would you change in the way you solved the problem?"

"What did you learn today?"

"Was it hard or easy to solve the problem today?"

"How do you feel when a task is difficult?"

To talk about what made a task hard or easy, students need to think. Practice helps them develop an awareness of their strategies, abilities, and limitations, and of the characteristics of the task. That awareness increases the probability that students will engage in monitoring their progress toward their goal when they solve a problem.

Such monitoring, in turn, increases even more their awareness of their own actions. It helps them realize the need to explore and analyze a problem, revise their strategies, and use alternative strategies.

Talking about what made a task hard or easy helps children talk about their feelings as well as their thoughts. When children are given the opportunity to hear their peers express their feelings, their own insecurities and feelings of self-doubt may be relieved. When you accept your students' feelings, they will begin to believe that their feelings are important and valid. Thus, they may begin to express themselves more freely. Further, children's sense of themselves as learners may be strengthened if they see that their feelings are taken into account by the teacher in shaping the curriculum.

Free expression of one's thoughts and feelings can be encouraged only in an atmosphere of unconditional acceptance like the one we have seen in Mary's classroom. In your classroom, try to find ways to let your students know that you are listening to them. Remember that body language tells a lot about what you think and how you feel. Show your students that you are interested in them and that you are listening to them. You are a model for your students. As you model acceptance, attentiveness, and respect, children learn to behave in a similar way.

In an accepting environment, children also learn that it is acceptable to be wrong, to need help from others, and to find a task difficult. Give feedback to your students. Appreciate their efforts and communicate your appreciation to them. Assess their progress and let them know how much they have grown.

To review, in order to teach your students how to reflect and talk about the experience of learning, follow these steps:

1. Arrange the seating to foster communication.
2. Tell your students that in this lesson they will talk about what it is like to work on solving a problem.
3. Motivate your students to talk about what they have done.
4. Ask your students questions that would help them think about and evaluate what they have done.
5. Show your students that you are interested in what they have to say.
6. Paraphrase or reflect what your students say.
7. Ask questions to clarify what your students are saying.
8. Involve all of your students in the discussion.
9. Show unconditional acceptance of your students' thoughts and feelings. Let them know that it is acceptable to be wrong.
10. Give your students feedback. Let them know that they are learning to do something that is difficult but very important.

▲ *What Comes Next?*

In the next chapter, as we look at ways to interview individual students in the classroom, we will discover the potential of individual interviews for both teaching and ongoing assessment.

CHAPTER THREE

▲ *Interviewing Individual Students*

Learning to ask good questions and to be a good listener is a process that takes time. Fortunately, interviewing skills can be learned "on the job." By starting with the simplest kinds of interviews, you and your students together can develop the skills needed to tackle more difficult techniques. Even from the beginning, both you and your students will benefit. Over time, with practice and reflection, you will achieve greater depth and power in your interviewing.

Most of the teachers with whom we have worked began with individual interviewing. Some went on to develop whole-class interviewing techniques. As you develop your interviewing skills, you may wish to use interviewing in whole-class situations as described in Chapter Four. But because it is easier to listen and respond to one voice than to many, it will be most productive for you to begin with individual interviewing strategies.

There are different types of individual interviews. In this chapter, we will look first at interviews that, although they may take place in the midst of the classroom setting, are conducted apart from the rest of the class. Then we will discuss examples of interviews, both spontaneous and planned, that are incorporated into whole-class activities.

Individual interviews apart from the class can be relatively structured, semi-structured, or flexible interviews. In a structured interview, the tasks and questions are planned in advance. The interview with Jennifer described in Chapter One may be called a flexible interview, because the interviewer's questioning responds in a flexible way to the behavior of the student. The semi-structured interview is like the structured interview in some ways and like the flexible interview in others. The tasks and questions are planned in advance, but the teacher can follow up on the student's responses in a flexible way.

Let us look at examples of each of the three types, beginning with the structured interview.

▲ Structured Individual Interview

For the beginner, structured interviews are a good place to start because they permit the interviewer to do most of the planning and much of the thinking ahead of time. As the teacher uses the same test over and over with different students, a proficiency develops, allowing the teacher to spend more energy observing and less energy thinking about what to say. But even though the tasks and questions are planned in advance, the structured interview, as we will see, is not as rigid as a standardized test.

Some of our teachers found it worthwhile once or twice a year to interview each child in the class in preparation for writing reports to parents. Information gained during the interview was up to date, detailed, and of great value when communicating to parents both the teachers' goals and their students' accomplishments.

Other teachers interviewed only those children about whom they wished to have a baseline of information: a child entering the class after the start of the year, or a child whose level of achievement was puzzling. Structured interviews helped them accomplish their purpose efficiently.

Let us look first at structured interviews with two kindergarten students. Their teacher, Laura, interviewed each student in her class in preparation for writing progress reports to parents.

What Laura Did

Laura began by reminding her students that each of them would be interviewed. She told them that she was interested to find out how they think about numbers and about math. Then she went on to ask each student to perform a set of tasks. To simplify the process of recording each interview, Laura had made a basic recording sheet that enabled her to compare the results of the fall and spring interviews for each student.

Laura used the same set of tasks as a basis for each interview. Tasks in her questionnaire included counting aloud, counting blocks, writing numerals, and performing simple addition and subtraction. Other tasks involved patterns, block towers, skip-counting, and attributes such as shape, size, and color.

What kinds of information could be gained with such a simple collection of tasks? As an example, let us look at the very informative results obtained when Laura interviewed two of her students, Manny and Carol.

We will take a look at their responses to three of the tasks that Laura had prepared: Write the numbers from 1 to 10, Roll two dice and find their sum, and Subtract one row of blocks from another.

Here are Manny and Carol's responses to the first task.

Write the numbers from 1 to 10 (Manny).

Teacher (T): *Write your numbers from 1 to 10.*

Manny (M): [Writes the numerals 1 through 3 and has difficulty forming the numeral 3 correctly.]

T: *Are you sure that your 3 is correct?*

M: [After two erasures, continues without difficulty to 10.]

T: *Can you go any higher?*

M: [Writes the numerals from 11 to 20, even forming the 3 in 13 correctly without any reminder.]

T: *How high can you count?*

M: [Counts to 109.] *That's all.*

Write the numbers from 1 to 10 (Carol).

T: *Write your numbers from 1 to 10.*

Carol (C): [Writes the numerals 1 through 10 and has difficulty forming the numeral 8 correctly.]

T: *Are you sure that your 8 is correct?*

C: [Erases and tries again twice, but with little improvement.]

T: *Can you go any higher?*

C: [Writes the numerals from 11 to 12 correctly but reverses the digits in the two-digit numbers 13 to 19.]

T: [Pointing to the 13] *Which comes first, the three or the one?*

C: [Corrects the 13 by switching the digits, and then corrects the remaining numerals.]

T: Can you make a 20?

C: No.

T: What numbers do you use to make a 20?

C: 0 and 2.

T: Which comes first, though?

C: 2. [Writes 20 correctly.]

Laura noticed that both students needed hints in order to write correctly the numerals from 1 to 20. Manny had difficulty with the numeral 3 and Carol had a similar difficulty with the numeral 8. But Carol reversed the digits in the two-digit numbers, whereas Manny did not. Carol was not confident of her ability to write the 20. Laura concluded that Carol needed more help than Manny did in order to be correct. This information was useful right away as Laura planned instruction for these two students, and later in the year when she interviewed them again to measure their progress.

In a strictly structured interview, exactly the same words are used for each student, and each student is given exactly the same tasks. But some relaxation of this strictness may provide more useful and more informative results. Notice that Laura used the same script as she interviewed each student but that she did not ask Carol to count aloud. Perhaps she had previously assessed Carol's ability to count aloud.

In a structured interview with many tasks, certain tasks may be skipped if they are too easy or too difficult for a particular student, or if those tasks recently have been presented in another context. Because the structured interview is less rigid than a standardized test, items may be omitted or adapted as appropriate for the individual student.

It is often useful to relax strictness in other ways, too. As Laura did, you will learn more about your students if you question further when a student seems to be unable to perform the task adequately. Perhaps the student is not trying hard or is distracted. Questions such as "Are you sure?" or "Can you go any higher?" prompt the child to try harder without giving any extra help.

A hint from the teacher may be enough to enable the student to improve his or her performance. For example, Laura asked Carol, "Which comes first, the 3 or the 1?" This was a hint that the order written was incorrect. Carol did not just correct the 13, however. She realized that an error in the 13 implied other errors, and she corrected them as well, demonstrating an ability to think abstractly about the position of the numerals even though she did not fully understand place value.

Laura's question—"Which comes first, the 3 or the 1?"—was a leading question. It told Carol exactly what her error was. It might have been better if Laura had waited until Carol was finished and then asked, "How would you write 31? How is that number different from 13? What does the 1 in this number [point to 31] stand for? What does the 1 in this number [point to 13] stand for?" In this way Laura would have helped Carol herself do the thinking as she worked through the process of understanding the reason for the placement of digits in a numeral.

Here is the second of the three tasks. Laura's student rolls two ordinary dice and is asked to name the sum of the two numbers rolled. The task may be repeated several times until Laura has a good idea of the student's addition strategies.

Roll two dice and find their sum (Manny).

M: [Rolls 5 and 1.]

T: What numbers did you get?

M: 5 and 1.

T: How much did you get all together?

M: 6. [Rolls again, gets 3 and 3.]

T: What did you get?

M: 6.

T: How did you get that so quickly?

M: I know that 3 and 3 is 6.

M: [Rolls 6 and 3.]

T: Now?

M: 9.

T: What did you say to yourself in your head?

M: 6, 7, 8, 9.

T: Again.

M: [Rolls again.] *11.*

M: [Rolls again.] *10.*

T: How did you know that?

M: Last time I got 6 and 5. This time I got 6 and 4, so it has to be 1 less.

Roll two dice and find their sum (Carol).

T: What did you get?

C: 3 and 5.

T: How much is that all together?

C: [Holds out 5 fingers on one hand, 3 on the other. After a long pause, she begins to count to herself.] 8.

T: Good. Roll again.

C: [Rolls 2 and 4. Counts, this time without hesitation.] 6.

T: How did you know that so quickly?

C: I counted on my fingers.

T: Roll again.

C: [Rolls two 5's.] 10.

T: How did you figure that out so quickly?

C: I know that 5 and 5 is 10.

T: Very good.

The very brief dice-rolling task revealed much information. Laura learned that Manny knows the "double," 3 plus 3, and he is able to use the strategy of counting on from the larger number when he counts on to find 6, 7, 8, 9. He is able to use one result to find a related one, as when he says that 6 plus 4 must be 1 less than 6 plus 5. Carol also knows at least one double, 5 plus 5. She is able to use finger counting to find the other sums. Although she is hesitant, she is accurate with this concrete method.

In this second task, you may have noticed that the script was not identical from one student to the next. Depending on what the student said and did, different questions were asked. When the answer came slowly, Laura said, "Good, roll again." When the answer came quickly, her response was "How did you get (know, figure out) that so quickly?" She elicited an explanation of their strategies by asking, "What did you say to yourself in your head?" and "How did you know that?"

Laura used observation, too. She observed Carol using finger counting and noted that on her recording sheet. You probably will have noticed that Manny and Carol were well able to describe addition strategies typical of kindergarten students.

Here is the final task in this series. It involved subtracting 7 from 11 with the help of small blocks. This was the most difficult of the three tasks and revealed the greatest difference between Laura's two students.

Subtract one row of blocks from another (Manny).

T: Make a row of eleven blocks.

M: [Does it quickly, choosing blocks after a quick glance.]

T: And another row of 7 blocks.

M: [Quickly makes another row beside the first.]

T: Which row is longer?

M: [Points to the longer row.] *This one.*

T: How much longer is it?

M: [He places the row with 7 blocks directly *under* the longer row, and pushes aside 7 in each row, then counts the remaining blocks.] *4.*

Subtract one row of blocks from another (Carol).

T: Make a row of 11 blocks.

C: [Does it, selecting the blocks very carefully, looking for certain pleasing colors, and rejecting blocks that are chipped or faded.]

T: And another row of 7 blocks.

C: [Again, does it carefully.]

T: Which row has more?

C: [Points to the row of 11 blocks.] *This one here.*

T: How many more?

C: [Shrugs shoulders.]

T: [Encouragingly] *You were right, there are 11 in this row* [pointing] *and 7 in this row. How many more are in the longer row?* [As Carol still seems not to respond, Laura pushes aside corresponding pairs of blocks, one by one, until 7 pairs of blocks have been pushed aside.] *1, 2, 3, 4, 5, 6, 7. How many are left in this row?* [Pointing to the short row.]

C: None.

T: How many in this row?

C: 4.

T: Very good.

In the block subtraction task, neither Manny nor Carol had any difficulty in making the rows of blocks and in saying that the row with 11 had more blocks than the row with 7. But Carol did not seem to understand the question "How many more?" whereas Manny competently performed a manual procedure for finding the difference.

You may have noticed that Laura was not consistent in her wording. She asked Manny which row was longer, but she asked Carol which row had more. Perhaps Laura asked Carol which row had more because she believed that in this way she was simplifying the task for Carol. Generally, in a structured interview it is best to start with the same language for each student. If a student seems not to understand the question or task at first, the wording can then be modified as needed to help the student understand.

Finally, Laura told Carol, "You were right, there are 11 in this row and 7 in this row." Perhaps she said this to encourage Carol because Carol was having difficulty with the question "How many more?" Usually it is possible to encourage students without telling them that they are right. Laura might simply have repeated Carol's words. "There are 11 in this row and 7 in this row."

Letting students know when they are right or wrong may give them the message that their goal is to get the teacher's approval and that the product of their work is more important than the process. In the interview, it is important to make clear that the process is of greatest importance to the teacher. The process reveals thinking strategies. The product does not tell the teacher very much about the student's understanding. Getting the right answer does not always imply understanding. In fact, it often is informative for the teacher to explore the thinking that underlies correct or right answers.

Based on the interviews described above, Laura decided that Carol needed more practice with finger addition as well as addition games with blocks, dominoes, pennies, and other concrete materials to develop her comfort with addition of small numbers before moving on to larger ones. Manny, she decided, was ready to extend his understanding of how different sums are related, and ready to work on remembering the combinations that have a sum of 10, in preparation for work with sums between 11 and 20.

Laura recorded her observation that Manny used the blocks as semi-abstract counters, interested only in their number and position, while Carol used them as individual, concrete objects, and concerned herself with their color and condition.

One of the authors soon afterward conducted an interview with Carol and another girl, using two- and three-dimensional geometric tasks with color block patterns. In that interview, Carol demonstrated geometric reasoning far more sophisticated than that of the other student whose arithmetical skills surpassed hers. Carol appears to have good visual thinking skills.

It is possible that Carol's understanding of number might be furthered by using two-dimensional patterns of tiles or blocks to represent numbers. Domino or playing card patterns as alternatives to rows of blocks might be of help to her. Perhaps pennies might be more meaningful than blocks for Carol. Laura might have considered testing her again with different materials, to see whether the result would be different.

It should also be noted that Carol had been recovering from a head cold on the day of the interview, and might have performed differently had she been in good health. Such temporary conditions often influence assessment results and should not be overlooked. Any teacher-made recording sheet should provide a generous area for comments indicating temporary conditions as well as ideas for possible further assessment and teaching strategies.

We have not yet considered one very important question: How did Laura find a time and a place to conduct individual structured interviews? Laura and several other teachers with whom we worked interviewed two or three students each day until all had been interviewed. They sat for the required fifteen minutes for each student at a desk or small table in the classroom while the rest of the class was occupied with quiet work. One teacher took a student desk and two chairs out into the hallway for this purpose, keeping an eye and an ear alert for disruptions within the classroom in her absence. Another teacher kept students for their brief interviews when the class was scheduled for a "special" such as art or gym class or from recess. Of course, if a teacher has an aide or assistant for part of the day, the job is simpler. The aide manages the class while the teacher interviews students.

What You Can Do

To take full advantage of a structured interview such as the ones described here, you need to base your set of tasks on your best understanding of the skills and knowledge that students need to have to succeed in your class. You should consider, as well, the sequence in which those skills and knowledge usually are learned. In other words, tasks that are important to your teaching goals will make the most useful set of interviewing tasks. Then you can build on what your students reveal during the interview to help you in planning how to teach.

Time spent in simplifying the wording of questions is well worthwhile. You want your students to understand what they are being asked to do. Probably you will need to revise your wording once or twice after using the interview questions a few times.

To record your observations quickly, you will save time if you use simple codes to represent common strategies and errors. For example, Laura might have used FC for finger counting, COL for counting on from the larger number, CA for counting all, D for doubles, RF for related fact, and DR for digit reversal. You can make up your own codes to represent strategies that your students use. When you give the student prompts or hints, they should be noted on the recording sheet. The letter "P" or "H" may be written next to the student's response if there is no time to write more than that. If you leave space for responses to two interviews on the same recording sheet, you can more easily compare the two interviews to assess growth over time.

Guidelines for conducting a flexible interview are to be found in Chapter 6. In addition to reading that chapter, you may wish to consider the following points:

- Make sure that you have all necessary materials ready before conducting the interview. You don't wish to disrupt the interview just because you need a few more blocks or the marker pen is dried out.

- Set up a table or desk with two chairs in a convenient place, perhaps in a corner of your classroom. Make sure that the student is comfortable as the interview begins. Start the tasks only after you have set the student at ease.

- Present each task clearly. If a student is not able to perform the task, you may repeat or rephrase the instructions or even give a prompt or a hint. Accept whatever the student says and does. Refrain from indicating to the student when an error has been made. Just move on to the next task.

After the interview, thank the student for participating.

Here is a brief list of guidelines that may help you prepare to conduct your own structured interviews with students in your class.

1. First decide what is the purpose of your structured interview.
2. List the tasks that you wish to include.

3. Determine the wording you wish to use as you ask questions.

4. Design a simple recording sheet that will let you record students' responses quickly.

5. Assemble any manipulative materials, marker pens, and other materials that you will need for the interviews.

6. Determine a time and a place for each interview.

7. In interviewing students:

   a. Introduce the student to the interview process; make the student comfortable.

   b. Present the tasks, making note on your record sheet of:
      • which tasks were presented.
      • the student's responses.
      • codes for strategies used.
      • prompts or hints given.
      • circumstances such as health, fatigue, noise in classroom, interruptions.

   c. Thank the student for doing a good job.

   d. Right away, record your comments and indications for follow-up instruction.

▲ A Semi-structured Individual Interview

A semi-structured interview may be used to assess a student in order to plan for individualized instruction. In contrast with the structured interview, which is more likely to be used in the same form for many students, the semi-structured interview is ideal for assessing a single student when the teacher has a specific question about that student. The task or tasks may be tailor-made for a particular situation. As the interview proceeds, the teacher may modify the tasks or even invent new ones on the spur of the moment, as needed. Let us look at one example of such an interview.

What Betty Did

Betty believed that her second-grade class as a whole understood simple subtraction problems quite well, so she was surprised and puzzled by one student's poor scores on standardized test questions in the spring of the year. She decided to conduct a semi-structured interview with this student, Gail, to investigate Gail's understanding of subtraction. Betty selected several test questions that Gail had missed, and presented them to her again in an individual interview lasting no more than about five minutes. Betty began by asking questions aloud.

> *Teacher (T): What's 10 minus 6?*
>
> *Gail (G): 4.*
>
> *T: What's 16 minus 7?*
>
> *G:* [After a long pause, during which Gail moves her fingers slightly] *9.*
>
> *T: How did you figure that out?*
>
> *G: I counted back.*
>
> *T: Very good.*

Betty invented some tasks not on the standardized test as she went along. Betty had observed that Gail was able to count down correctly. She had observed that Gail used her fingers to keep track of the counting. She wanted to see whether Gail would try to use that same strategy or would use a different strategy when the difference between the two numbers was greater than 10, the number of her fingers. The next problem on the standardized test was not appropriate because the difference was much too great to make counting down a reasonable strategy. So she invented a new problem which was more to her purpose.

> *T: Now, what's 29 minus 17?* [After a very long pause during which Gail did not seem to be counting, but was becoming uncomfortable] *You can use paper and pencil if you like.*
>
> *G:* [Makes tally marks. Has trouble making 29 marks, more trouble taking 17 of them away.] *It's 15.*
>
> *T: What if we wrote it this way?* [Writes it vertically, with the 17 under the 29.]
>
> *G:* [Writes 1 in the tens column and 5 in the ones column. Erases the 5 and replaces it with a 2, after counting down using her fingers.] *12.*

Betty had learned quite a bit about Gail from this brief section of the dialogue. Gail knew, for example, that tally marks could be used to represent a subtraction problem, although she was not able to use them successfully for such a large number as 29. She knew something about column subtraction but began in the tens column. In this case, the answer was not affected because the problem did not require regrouping or borrowing. Gail did not remember the basic fact 9 − 7 and had to count down to find the answer.

Perhaps you will have noticed that in a semi-structured interview such as this one, the interviewer is entirely free to give hints and prompts of any kind. In our example, Betty simply wanted to find out what Gail knew about subtraction so that she could help her. Fairness to other classmates was not an issue here because Gail was not being compared with any other student.

Let's see how Betty and Gail concluded their very brief interview.

> *T: What's 43 − 6?*
>
> *G:* [Gail is now looking over at the test questions and anticipates this one.] *Oh, I knew that. I just knew 43 − 3 and then we do another 3, so it's 36.*
>
> *T:* [Again reading from the test.] *What's 42 − 9?*
>
> *G:* [Quickly but not very confidently] *2 − 9 is 7, and 4. 47.*
>
> *T: Does that make sense?*
>
> *G: No.*
>
> *T: Why not?*
>
> *G: I don't know. Can I count backwards?*
>
> *T: Yes, of course.*
>
> *G: 42, 41, 40, 39, 38, 37, 36, 35, 34. 34.*
>
> *T: Very good. Thank you, Gail.*

You may have been bothered by Betty's ignoring Gail's errors here. Betty did not correct them or even comment on them. Twice, she just went right on as though there had been no errors. It may be that Betty was satisfied with the information that she had gained from the errors.

On the other hand, she could have urged Gail to check her work by asking, "How did you figure that out? Take your time. Don't rush." Perhaps Gail was rushing and would have given the correct answer on the second try. Remember that there is no one right way to conduct this interview. Even Betty might shape it differently if it had to be done over again.

Let's return once more to Gail. Gail again had subtracted the smaller number from the larger in each column. This time it did matter, because the problem required regrouping, or borrowing. Betty asked Gail if her answer made sense. Gail replied, "No," probably because if it had made sense, her teacher would not have asked her. "Does that make sense?" probably was interpreted to mean "Your answer is not correct." It is not likely that sense-making with regard to subtraction is something that Gail has had much opportunity to experience. Instead of asking whether the answer made sense, it might have been better for Gail to emphasize the process rather than the product by asking, "How did you figure that out?" or "Can you prove your answer?" In trying to answer one of these questions, Gail might discover her own error and perhaps even discover a way to improve her subtraction strategies.

Finally, Gail asks to use the only strategy with which she is comfortable, counting down. Unfortunately, she does not use counting down correctly in this case.

From this one short interview, Betty learned that Gail's skills were much weaker than she had realized. The interview revealed that the only method Gail felt she could rely on was counting down, and she was unable to use even that method with guaranteed success. She was unable to draw and count tally marks well enough to use them successfully. When using the standard algorithm, she began on the left instead of in the ones column, and she subtracted the smaller digit from the larger, regardless of its position. She did not expect her answers to make sense to her. Indeed, the entire subtraction process did not make sense to her.

Gail appeared to her teacher to be in a hurry, making stabs in the dark for many of her answers. It is important that such students be given enough time to think through what they are doing. Rather than being asked to complete a specified number of problems on a given day, it would be better for her to understand a few problems well, in order to develop confidence in her work. Gail needs typical first-grade work with manipulatives, with basic facts, and with place value. To require her to go on with more difficult subtraction problems such as those on the standardized test would only frustrate her and increase her reliance on guesswork and luck.

Gail's teacher had not yet explored in a systematic way any of the weaknesses that Gail had revealed to her. Further questioning might help Betty discover what her student knew about place value and which basic facts she did know.

More meaningful tasks would reveal whether Gail could solve problems relating to situations that were important to her. It would be interesting to know, for example, whether Gail would be better able to solve the same problems if they were presented in the context of spending money and receiving change.

Betty's interview with Gail was one of the first she had ever attempted, yet it revealed surprising information that would help her design more appropriate instruction.

What You Can Do

You, too, can learn to diagnose the needs of your students in this way. Any situation that stimulates your interest and concern can be a topic for your interview. Standardized test questions are not the only source of tasks available. Other sources may include teacher-made test questions, problems worked in class, textbook problems, comments and questions from students, and problems that arise from meaningful situations shared by students.

It is often useful to invent tasks for a special purpose as you go along. As you try to interpret your student's successes and failures, you develop a hunch to explain them. To test that hunch, you may need a particular task that you could not have anticipated in advance of the interview. You are free to set the tasks and respond to the student as you think best. There are no fixed rules. The only essential rule and the hardest one to follow is for you to learn from the student, rather than to teach the student. This is not the time to tell the student what to do or how to do it. If you want to advance the student's thinking, ask questions to help him or her construct the new meaning, concept, or skill.

Remember that although you are free to give hints and prompts and to help your student over hurdles, you do not need to help your student come to a right answer. Do whatever you need to help you understand your student. You will then be able to custom-tailor the teaching that comes afterward. Your goal is to be better equipped to guide your students as they learn mathematical thinking skills.

It is not necessary to create a special recording sheet for this kind of interview, although you probably will wish to record your comments and indications for future instruction.

Here is a set of guidelines that may help you get started with your own semi-structured interviews.

1. Select a student and an area of inquiry.

2. Choose tasks that will help you diagnose your student's needs.

3. Make an educated guess regarding your student's thinking.

4. Ask questions to check that guess.

5. If necessary, revise it and ask more questions.

6. When you wish to see if prompts or hints will help, offer them.

7. Do not be afraid of student mistakes. Learn from them. When your student fails to answer a question correctly, try to avoid walking the student through the problem in order to arrive at a correct answer.

8. Use the information you have gained to plan for further instruction.

▲ The Flexible Interview

The most difficult and the most time-consuming of individual interviews is the flexible interview. It is also the most exciting and the most rewarding. As we have seen, the flexible interview resembles the "clinical interviews" by means of which Piaget gained so much of his understanding of children's thinking.

Teachers without classroom assistants or aides will probably not be able to afford the time required for such an interview with each and every student in the class. But in the case of the student who in some way remains a mystery to the teacher, the problem student, or the new student entering in the middle of the school year, this interview can provide more information in twenty valuable minutes than weeks of observation in the classroom setting.

It can also be a teacher's research tool. It is of great value to the teacher who wishes to know what her "average, typical" student knows and thinks, not just how he or she performs. Such an interview can lead to a deeper understanding of how students at her grade level think when they do math, and what form their concepts and beliefs take.

The topic and purpose of the flexible interview may be determined in advance, but flexible interviews are more open ended than the topic and purpose of the semi-structured interview.

In our semi-structured example, the original purpose was to find out why Gail did poorly with the subtraction problems on a standardized test. The tasks were all either questions from the standardized test or other, similar questions.

In our example of flexible interviewing, the purpose was less specific. The teacher wanted to find out what a first-grade student knew about three-digit numbers. She had prepared an initial open-ended task using base ten blocks and planned to continue after that first task by responding to what her student said and did. She had no map of the interview laid out in advance. She would follow the student's lead and see where it took them. Their interview would last twenty minutes. We will look at a small part of it.

What Clara Did

Clara's first-grade students had been using base ten blocks to represent numbers in the tens and the hundreds. One of them, Brian, seemed to have difficulty with naming and writing numbers greater than 100. Clara wished to interview Brian to investigate his understanding of number names and symbols as they are related to place value.

She decided to present him with combinations of base ten blocks and ask him to tell her what numbers they represented. She planned to begin with numbers that are less than 100 and then go on to numbers that are greater. She planned to listen and observe him closely, to see if she could discover what caused his difficulties. She had no more specific plans than that. Let's see what happened in Clara's interview with Brian:

> *Teacher (T):* [Puts a square flat block on the mat.] *What is that number on your mat?*
>
> *Brian (B): A hundred.*
>
> *T:* [Puts 8 long blocks, or rods, on the mat.] *And that?*
>
> *B: 80.*
>
> *T: How much is that total number on your mat?*
>
> *B: 80 a hundred.*

Now, Clara had heard what he said, but she did not know what he was thinking when he said it, so she was unable to help him go beyond this way of thinking. She might have been tempted to correct him by saying simply, "No, we call that number 180. First we say the number of hundreds and then we say the number in the tens place." He would quite possibly have been confused for a while, using both forms, his and hers, until finally he would have given up the unconventional, personal (incorrect) form.

However, she was letting him lead the dialogue and she was learning from him. Being very, very flexible, she did not even catch her breath, frown, or clear her throat! Let us see what happened next.

T: 80 a hundred. Can you write 80 a hundred?

B: [Writes 80   100.]

T: All right. 80 a hundred, that's what you're saying? Can you count that? Can you show me how you count what's on your mat to know how much that is?

Without telling Brian anything, she offered him two strategies with which he should have felt comfortable, writing and counting. At first, this might seem to have been an end run around the issue. Looking at her questions in a more positive light, she wanted to see whether Brian would be able to write or count to 180 correctly, even though he could not arrive at it by combining the 100 and the 80. Now let's see what happened next.

B: [Pointing to the hundred] *That's a hundred, and then* [pointing to the tens] *2, 4, 6, 8. All of these are tens. So I know it's 80 a hundred.*

T: Now, you have 80 in your rods, and 100 in your flats. Now, can you put them together and write how much they are all together?

B: Yes, count them.

T: Right. Now, can you count them, together?

B: I would go like this [Putting each tens rod on top of the flat hundreds block, counting each tens rod followed by the row of ten on the flat block beneath it] *10 20, 30 40, 50 60, 70 80, 90 100, 110 120, 130 140, 150 160.* [He does not count the two uncovered rows of ten.]

At this point, what would you have done next, if you had been interviewing Brian? Would you have pointed out the two uncovered and uncounted rows of ten? Would you have asked him, "Are you sure that you have counted everything?" Notice that although she used the word *together* twice, it seemed to have made little impact on Brian's thinking. Wishing Brian to do the thinking for himself, Clara only showed that she still was listening for a better way.

T: Mmm. Hmm.

B: [After a pause] *Wait!* [Again counts each rod followed by a corresponding row of units on the hundreds block, this time without actually laying the rods on the hundreds block; but before finishing, he pauses again for a while, thinking.] *Oh, so a simpler way would be . . .*

T: Yes, I would like to know a simpler way.

B: [Counting first the hundred, then the tens rods] *100, 110, 120, . . . 170, 180.*

T: So what number is that?

B: [With some surprise] *180!*

T: O.K. Can you write it?

B: [Writes 180.]

Clara's patience was rewarded. Not only did she discover the source of Ben's difficulty, he also was able to discover it himself.

It often happens that skills learned by rote are not connected with skills that make sense, that are well understood. Ben knew how to count aloud by 10's beyond 100 and how to write those numbers as well. Those were rote skills. He also knew that 80 and 100 could be combined. But he never had connected the number 180 with the quantity that is the combination of 80 and 100. Suddenly he made the connection, by following a logical path of his own invention.

Not all flexible interviews end with this flash of understanding on the part of the student. Most do not. But teachers tell us that they are amazed by what they themselves discover when they become the students and allow their students to be the teachers. In the flexible interview it becomes very apparent that teaching is not "telling." Here, where teaching and assessment are so closely linked, teaching sometimes is listening.

What You Can Do

Remember to refer to the interviewing guidelines in Chapter 6. In addition to suggestions in that chapter, here are some suggestions specifically related to your needs in the classroom.

How will you find the time and place for flexible interviews?

Some teachers manage to conduct clinical interviews before or after school or during lunch or recess time. Others find a way to interview students at a table in a corner of the classroom or at a small desk in the hallway just outside the classroom, while the class is occupied with quiet work. If there is an aide who can manage the rest of the class, the interview may take place in the library or other quiet area.

What about selecting tasks for the flexible interview?

In our example, Clara had prepared only one task for Brian. In fact, she had already used a similar initial task with each of several other students in her class.

When you yourself prepare for an interview, it is wise to prepare more than one task. Plan a task that you think is at your student's level, one that is too easy, and one to provide extra challenge. Often you will be surprised to find that your student knows quite a bit more or quite a bit less than you had anticipated about the topic that you have selected.

First, it is wise to begin with a task that you think is too easy. If you have overestimated the student, the easy task may be challenging enough. If the first task is indeed too easy, your student will soon become confident with the easy task, and then you can move to something more difficult. Second, your first task may not work as well as you hope. Then you have an alternative or two available. Be sure that you have at hand all the materials needed for each of the tasks.

Not every interview need begin with a task at all. Some begin with a question. With a student new to your class, for example, you might begin a very interesting and informative interview with questions like: "What do you like most about math?" or "Is there anything you don't like about math?" or "What would you like to know about math?" or "What did you learn today in math?" If followed up with a question such as: "Why do you think that is? Can you explain it to me?" or "Can you show me with pencil and paper?" or "Can you show me with these tiles?" you may get helpful information about a student that you would not expect or even know how to ask for.

Manipulatives help the student think and can also foster communication. They can help the student make mathematical thinking explicit, getting the ideas out where they can be seen when words alone are not adequate. If the student will be writing, provide a marker pen rather than a pencil so you can more easily read and interpret what your student writes.

In her interview, Clara used base ten blocks because her students already were familiar with them from their work in class. You may wish to use familiar materials, too, because you can build on that familiarity. Sometimes, however, you will want to select a new activity using unfamiliar materials. Your students will find their novelty interesting. Very young children often enjoy tasks that involve small toys, trucks, or amusing dolls.

Will your students object to being taken aside for an interview?

Far from resenting the time taken from other classroom activities, students enjoy that rare commodity, the undivided attention of the teacher, and often are disappointed when their time is up.

Finally, enjoy the interview. For its duration, forget about direct instruction and learn from your students. Your teaching will be refreshed and renewed by what you learn.

If you wish to conduct a flexible interview with one of your students, you may find the following guidelines helpful.

1. Plan a time and place for the interview.
2. Assemble all necessary materials.
3. Welcome the student and make the student comfortable.
4. Explain simply the purpose of the interview.
5. Prepare to listen and observe closely.
6. Present the first task.
7. Be responsive. Listen and ask. Do not tell.
8. Ask questions that are nondirective: "Can you explain that?" "How did you figure it out?" "Can you show me how you did it?" "How would you explain it to a friend?"
9. Ask questions whether the student is right or wrong. You may get information either way.
10. If the task is too easy or does not work, or the student is losing interest, present the task in a different way or with different manipulative materials, or switch to a different task altogether.
11. At the end of the interview, thank the student.

▲ *Spontaneous Questioning*

So far we have looked at interviews conducted apart from the context of the ongoing work of the classroom. The final two types of interview examined in this chapter are embedded in classroom activity. The first is entirely spontaneous. The second, questioning about a piece of work, may be spontaneous or it may be scheduled.

Most teachers already may be conducting the simplest kind of spontaneous interview. It can happen at any time. Without prior planning, the teacher's attention is shifted briefly away from the class as a whole, and is focused on an individual student. Perhaps this happens when a teacher notices something unexpected in a student's written work, or perhaps the teacher interrupts a class discussion to help a student in difficulty. It could also be that the teacher wishes to use a student's work as an example for others. We will look at three short examples of this type of interview.

What Some Teachers Did

First Scenario

Barbara had announced a problem to the class. She walked around the room while observing her students working. She noticed that one student had made an error that would prevent success with that problem, and she wished to help him past that difficulty so that he might move on with the class to the main elements of the lesson she had planned. And she wanted to do that quickly, because she did not wish to interrupt the other students in their work.

This is what she did:

Teacher (T): *Here's a problem. Our class has 24 children present today. Mrs. Bond has 19 in her classroom. How many more do we have?*

Alex (A): [Writes 24 and 91.]

T: [Noticing that Alex has reversed the numerals] *Nice Mrs. Bond would go crazy if she had 91 children.*

A: [Writes 19.]

T: *Why did you change your number?*

A: *Because I'm writing 19 and I have to put the 1 first.*

T: *Very good.*

The teacher saw that Alex was able to correct his digit-reversal error as soon as it was called to his attention. That was not enough. She wished to engage Alex in a brief dialogue that would allow her to decide whether he really understood the reason for his correction. She asked him to explain it. As he explained, he rehearsed the correct procedure. This rehearsal may help him remember how to write such a number correctly at another time.

Second Scenario

Our second spontaneous interview took place at the end of the school year. Ken, hoping to assess his students' understanding of place value, asked his first graders to write the largest number that they knew. When he noticed that John had written the numeral 10, he was surprised because he had expected John to write a much larger number. While other students were writing, he questioned John individually.

The following interview took place:

John (J): [Writes 10.]

Teacher (T): *John, can you write a three-digit number?*

J: [Writes 341.]

T: What's the number?

J: 341.

T: That's bigger than 10. How much bigger is 341 than 10?

J: 241. [Then, after a long pause] *O.K., 331.*

T: How did you figure it out?

J: I left the hundreds alone and I took a ten from the 40 and that makes 30 and I didn't bother with the ones either so that makes 331.

T: Very good, John.

The teacher had expected this student to write a number much higher than 10. He did not get involved in a confrontation about whether John could, in fact, write a larger number. By asking a different, more specific question, he gave up his original goal of discovering the largest number that John could write. He did manage to focus John's attention on the task. Because the teacher was primarily interested in how well John understood place value, he also accomplished his original goal.

Notice that the teacher did not respond immediately to John's incorrect answer to the question. Perhaps his silence suggested to John that he did not agree with the answer given. Although John's second answer was correct, the teacher continued to question him. He wished to find out how confident John was of his answer, what strategy he had used to arrive at it, and how well John would be able to explain his strategy.

In the vignettes we have just seen, the teachers persisted with the spontaneous interview after the student had performed the correction or the desired task. In each case the teacher asked for an explanation from the student of what he had done. Compliance was not the major goal of these teachers. Their major goals were understanding and communication—teaching and assessment.

Third Scenario

Now let us look at a different scenario. It is hardly long enough to be called an interview, but nonetheless it is a valuable dialogue between teacher and student. Here, students were engaged in sharing subtraction strategies in a classroom discussion. The problem to be solved was $36 - 10$.

Marcia had asked her class to share strategies in "mental" subtraction without using paper and pencil. One student, Carol, had had difficulty explaining her strategy to the class. The teacher wished to help Carol without holding up the flow of the discussion.

Marcia sensed that Carol was unable to explain her thoughts and was frustrated by the attempt. To give Carol time to think and to avoid embarrassment for her, the teacher sympathetically gave dignified expression to Carol's predicament.

> **Teacher (T):** *You are struggling to find a way to say what you did. Perhaps you're excited. But you're on the right track. Listen to the others now. Perhaps you'll hear something that will help you out.* [Calls on other students.]
> [A few minutes later] *Here's another problem: $67 - 10$. Who has an interesting strategy?*
>
> **Carol:** [She raises her hand and is called on.] *$7 + 3 = 10$.* [Counts on] *7. 8, 9, 10. Then $67 - 7 = 60$. So $60 - 3 = 57$.*
>
> **T:** *A great strategy. I followed you completely.*

In these two very brief exchanges, the teacher let Carol know that what she was doing was difficult but worth trying again. She urged Carol to continue to learn from the discussion with her classmates, and suggested that she would succeed eventually. Indeed, a few minutes later Carol again explained the same strategy, this time successfully. Here, the lesson taught was that personal struggle with math is eventually rewarded, and that an individual student's thinking is important and worthy of attention and respect. Notice, too, that Marcia's communication with Carol did not break the flow of the class. Rather, it enriched the discussion for Carol's classmates.

Each of these three scenarios is different, yet they share certain features. In each case the student did not meet the teacher's expectations. The teacher wished to resolve the situation without interrupting the flow of the class. The teacher was not satisfied with successful performance alone. She extended the dialogue to teach, to assess, to involve the student actively, and to facilitate the student's movement through the difficulty, rather than just past or around it. Those students received a message that the teacher valued not just compliant behavior but, more important, the thinking of each individual student.

What You Can Do

In your classroom, whenever a student has difficulty during shared group discussion, you have an opportunity to help that student and others who share the same difficulty. Think of those students as your keys to your class. You can ignore them and continue the lesson without them, or you can use their confusions to your advantage to motivate and to assess your class.

Your students will be motivated as they learn that every one of them is important to you and that your expectations for all of them are high. You expect all of them, not just the quickest and the most obedient, to succeed.

As you interview those in difficulty, you will learn in more detail about the obstacles that confront your students as they learn math. You will add to your store of information about the topic you are teaching and about how students come to understand that topic. And you will have the chance to try out new teaching strategies to see which ones work for which students. All these advantages cost only a very few minutes. In our examples, very few words were exchanged but, for each of the students involved, those few words meant the difference between success on the one hand and possible failure and withdrawal on the other hand. A very short interview at just the right moment is a powerful and efficient teaching tool.

Notice some of the strategies that our three teachers used. They let students know that they had noticed the students' difficulties. They sent the message that difficulty and hard thinking are acceptable in mathematics class. They did not rush their students. They gave them time to think. When necessary, they gave hints or prompts. They helped the students reenter the class discussion, and they rewarded them with congratulations.

Here are some guidelines that may assist you in your efforts to conduct spontaneous interviews like the three described above.

First Scenario

1. You notice a student in difficulty.
2. Let the student know that you recognize the difficulty.
3. If the student overcomes the difficulty without further help, ask for an explanation of how this was accomplished.
4. Express your satisfaction in some way.

Second Scenario

1. You notice something that does not agree with your current assessment of a child's level of understanding.
2. Let the student know that he has written something that you did not expect.
3. If the student still does not perform the task adequately, rephrase the instructions, give a hint, or modify the task.
4. Give plenty of time. Let the student think.
5. Ask the student to explain how he did the work.
6. Praise the student.

Third Scenario

1. You notice that a student is struggling to express her thoughts.
2. Let the student know that the struggle is worthwhile, though difficult, and that you expect her to achieve success after additional thought.
3. Urge the student to remain an active listener in the discussion while other students share their ideas.
4. Keep an eye on the student. Notice when the student wishes to speak again, and call on her if she offers to speak. Help the student reenter the discussion.
5. Congratulate the student when the difficult explanation has been successfully accomplished.

▲ *Questioning about a Piece of Work*

A different type of interview may be planned when the teacher interviews a student regarding work on a long-term problem or an assignment. Individual performance assessments may be of this type. Alternatively, the teacher and student together may review a project, journal entry, or portfolio item. This type of interview need not be a public presentation. It may be conducted at any time when the rest of the class is engaged in quiet work.

In the next example, two students were interviewed together because they had been assigned to work together on a project. As you will see, however, they did not really work together, but side by side. Their interview began as a pair of side-by-side individual interviews, but as it continued, they began to listen to each other.

What Kate Did

Pairs of students have been working for several days on a problem that is quite difficult for second graders who have had no formal instruction in multiplication. Now Sarah and Ben are being interviewed to assess their progress and their understanding of the problem. We will look only at the first segment of the rather long interview.

Teacher (T): Let's find all the papers you've been working with. Is that all?

Ben (B): We need that roll of papers over there.

T: Now, are you ready? Do you remember the problem? There are 12 packs of bubblegum cards. Each pack has 15 cards in it. How many cards altogether?

B: We got 107.

T: How did you get that?

Sarah (S): [Interrupting] *I went 15 + 15 + 15 + 15 + we went 15 12 times because there are 15 cards in each pack and 12 packs and I got 120.*

B: We decided to use rods [Dienes wood blocks: the tens block]. *I started counting and then I took 10 and 10 and 10.*

T: [Gets a box of base ten blocks.] *Can you show me what you've done?*

B: [Lays out 10 rods and 7 units. He overlaps each pair of rods to make a length equal to 15.]

T: [To Ben] *Can you show me all 12 packs?*

T: [To Sarah] *Maybe you can show it to me a different way.* [Sarah sets out 12 groups, each with 1 rod and 5 units. Ben continues to find his model too difficult to use. The overlapped rods are difficult to measure and count.]

T: [To Ben] *Can you count it out loud for me?*

B: *Well, I know that 15 plus 15 equals 30, then another 30 equals 60. So it's 107.*

T: *O.K. So you're convinced it's 107. Sarah, show me your way.*

S: *12 10's, 10, 20, 30, . . . 110, 120 and twelve 5's, 125, 130, 135, 140, . . . 175, 180.*

T: *Now you have three answers, 107, 120, and 180. Which one do you think is correct?*

B: *Our first answer was 107, and we heard someone else say it. It's really 180.*

S: *It's 180.*

T: *So you're both convinced that the answer is 180?*

S and B: *Yes.*

The interview had provided Kate with much information about her two students.

Ben revealed persistence, flexibility, and honesty, all useful in mathematics. He evidently knew that 15 could be represented as one and a half tens blocks (rods). He persisted with a difficult counting strategy because he knew that it modeled the problem correctly, even if he could not make it work. Ben honestly stated that he felt sure of his answer because he had heard other students say it. Later, he recognized the value of Sarah's model and changed his mind.

Sarah's use of 1 ten rod and 5 units to represent each pack of 15 cards was easier to count than Ben's overlapping rods, but at first she forgot to count the units.

We have seen that both Sarah and Ben understood multiplication as repeated addition. Each was able to relate written work to an oral explanation. Each knew a strategy for using base ten blocks to represent the bubblegum cards. In addition, Kate noticed that even after several days of working together on this problem, Ben and Sarah were working separately rather than collaboratively. All of this information would help her to plan for future instruction.

What You Can Do

The interview we have just reviewed involved two students. If you were to conduct an interview with a single student, your interview would follow the same general pattern. As mentioned, you may use such an interview to assess any performance, project, journal entry or other written work, or portfolio items.

Before the interview, be sure to give your student some advance notice so that there is time to gather work and materials together. To begin the interview, sit down and review the assignment. Let the student present the work that has been done before you begin asking questions.

The key to success is to encourage the student to present as you, the teacher, serve as the audience. Sit back and listen while the student makes the presentation.

Although you are respectful, you are not an unthinking audience. Gently question the student's method and challenge his conclusions. If the student is correct, challenge will strengthen his beliefs and his confidence. If the student is not correct, reflection and reexamination of the work may enable him to come to a new and better understanding. If more work is required, help the student formulate a plan for additional work. Finally, give the student the respect and congratulations that reward hard work.

If you wish to interview a student about a piece of work, you may wish to follow these guidelines:

1. Students have been working on a problem or project.
2. Arrange a time for the interview when the rest of the class will be busy working independently on the same problem or project.
3. Make sure that all of the necessary materials are together in one place.
4. Restate the problem to focus the student's attention on it.
5. Ask the student to report on work that has been accomplished.
6. Question further with open-ended questions, such as: "Can you show me how you did it?" "Can you do it out loud for me?" "Are you sure your answer is correct?"
7. Bring the interview to a conclusion by eliciting a final statement from the student.
8. If more work is required, plan with the student what the next steps will be.

▲ *What Comes Next?*

In the next chapter, the ideas we have been discussing with regard to individual interviews will be extended to interviews with the whole class. Chapter 4 will describe whole-class interviews themselves and their potential for both teaching and ongoing assessment.

CHAPTER FOUR

▲ *Interviewing Groups of Students in a Classroom Setting*

In the previous chapter we saw how we can use interviews to assess individual students both apart from the class and in the context of ongoing classroom activity. In this chapter we will look at strategies for interviewing clusters of students and for embedding interview techniques into whole-class discussion.

Teachers who interview groups of students are often surprised to discover how well group interviewing techniques help them to learn about an individual student in the group setting by doing the following:

- Assessing a student's mathematical thinking and understanding
- Assessing the student's skills in working within a group

You can learn about the group as a whole by doing the following:

- Assessing mathematical understanding, skills, and beliefs within the group as a whole
- Identifying social, cognitive, and metacognitive roles and relationships within the group

There are many ways to structure interviews in group situations. We will begin by looking at a third-grade teacher who interviews clusters of individual students at the blackboard.

▲ *Interviewing Clusters of Students*

A cluster interview is a sequence of individual interviews set within the context of a lesson. Cluster interviews provide both teacher and students with a transition from the now familiar individual interview toward more inclusive group interviews.

Cluster interviews are useful when students are ready to share individual work. Perhaps you have assigned seat work, and students have used a variety of strategies for that work. You wish the class to benefit from sharing their different strategies, so you and the class interview small groups of students about what they did and what they thought while they were doing it.

Several different goals are accomplished by this cluster interview technique. The teacher has an opportunity to assess the work of several individual students in a short period of time. The students benefit as well. They are able to compare and relate the different problem-solving strategies displayed side by side on the board. By relating different ways to approach a problem, students deepen their mathematical understanding of that problem and others like it. Finally, as students benefit from examining another's thinking strategies, they also learn to value communication with one another.

What Karen Did

Let us see how Karen, a third-grade teacher, incorporated cluster interviews into a lesson on multiplication. On the board she wrote the problem: multiply 4×23. This was a simple multiplication example, but challenging enough for Karen's class because they had not yet been taught a standard algorithm to solve it. Then Karen asked her class to develop their own strategies for solving the problem. As her students were working at their seats, she walked from desk to desk, observing their work. Sometimes she offered questions or comments. All the time, she was making decisions about whom to select for the cluster interviews.

After Karen had selected four students with different strategies and had noticed that most of the class had finished the exercise, she went to the front of the room to mark off the blackboard with vertical lines into four separate partitions. Finally, she called on the four students she had selected. Let's watch this cluster interview in action:

Teacher (T): Let's see, I'd like Patty, Ray, Joan, and . . . how about Nick to come to the board.

Patty, Ray, Joan, and Nick walked to the board, papers in hand, and copied their strategies there, each in one of the marked-off partitions. Here is what Karen's students wrote on the board:

Ray's method

$$\begin{array}{r} 23 \\ 23 \\ +23 \\ \hline 69 \end{array} \qquad \begin{array}{r} 69 \\ +23 \\ \hline 92 \end{array}$$

$$\begin{array}{r} 23 \\ 23 \\ 23 \\ +23 \\ \hline 92 \end{array}$$

Patty's method

$$\begin{array}{r} \overset{1}{2}3 \\ \times\ 4 \\ \hline 92 \end{array}$$

Joan's method

$$\begin{array}{r} 20 \\ \times 4 \\ \hline 80 \end{array} \qquad \begin{array}{r} 3 \\ \times 4 \\ \hline 12 \end{array} \qquad \begin{array}{r} 0 \\ \times 4 \\ \hline 0 \end{array}$$

$$\begin{array}{r} 80 \\ 12 \\ +\ 0 \\ \hline 92 \end{array}$$

Nick's method

$$\begin{array}{r} 25 \\ \times 4 \\ \hline 100 \end{array}$$

25 is 2 more than 23

I took away 2 from all of them
2, 4, 6, 8

100 − 8 = 92

Notice that Karen's students use the word *method* instead of *strategy*. It makes little difference whether your students call it a *method*, a *strategy*, or a *way* to solve the problem. What matters for all of us is that students are aware that there are many *different* methods, or strategies, or ways to solve a single problem.

Next Karen began to interview the students, one at a time, calling on students from left to right.

Teacher (T): All right, let's hear from all of you. Ray, go ahead.

Ray (R): 23 + 23 + 23 is 69. That's 3 × 23 and then 1 more is 92.

T: Good. Does anyone have any questions for Ray? No? Then, Ray, I have a question for you. Why did you choose to use 3 23's instead of 4?

R: I can do it with 4, too. I can write 4. [Writes a list of four 23's and adds them up, getting 92.] 4 × 3 is 12 [Writes 2.], 2, 4, 6, 8, 12. and 1 is 9. So 92. [Writes 9.]

T: Great.

Notice that Karen did not let Ray's presentation go without a question. No student had a question for him, so Karen asked one.

In addition to giving Ray the satisfaction of speaking, Karen learned something from Ray's answer to her question: she learned about Ray's flexibility in working with the distributive property.

Why had Karen selected Ray to go to the board? Her class already knew that multiplication can be thought of as repeated addition. Ray's method demonstrated an important property: that repeated addition works no matter how the numbers are grouped before they are added. Ray apparently had chosen to work with 3 23's instead of 4 23's in order to have a unique method. He knew from prior experience that uniqueness would give him a better chance to be selected to go to the blackboard.

The next student, Patty, presented Karen with a common and potentially difficult situation. Let's see how Karen and the class responded.

> ***Teacher (T):*** *Go ahead, Patty.*
>
> ***Patty (P):*** *[Who has learned the standard algorithm by rote from an older sister at home] I did it the quick way. I took 4 × 3 is 12 and then 4 × 2 is 8, plus I had 1, so I got 92.*
>
> ***T:*** *Any questions?*
>
> ***Charles (C):*** *[Trying to make sense of Patty's method] I don't understand the quick way. How did she do it?*
>
> ***T:*** *Can you explain your method? How did you do it?*
>
> ***P:*** *4 × 3 is 12. And 4 × 2 is 8, and 1 more makes 9. That's 92.*
>
> ***C:*** *I still don't get it. I can't write it that way.*
>
> ***T:*** *You know, it's hard to write something you don't understand. It's O.K. You will understand it pretty soon.*

Notice that although Karen accepted Patty's use of the standard algorithm, students who did not understand it were not convinced. Karen had taught her class to believe that math should make sense, and Patty's method seemed almost magical to students who had not yet learned it. Charles was honest enough to say that Patty's method did not make sense to him. He requested an explanation. When Patty was asked to explain her method, however, she could only repeat a description of the steps she had performed, since she, herself, did not understand why it worked.

Karen knew that all of her students would soon learn Patty's method, when they had finished their exploration of alternative methods. Then they—and Patty, too—would have a deeper understanding of how Patty's method works. For that reason, she did not push the class into a premature consideration of the standard algorithm.

She went on to question the next student, Joan.

Teacher (T): Joan? Let's have a look at your method.

Joan (J): Well, 20 × 4 is 80, 3 × 4 is 12, 0 × 4 is 0, and 80 + 12 + 0 is 92.

T: O.K. Who has a question for Joan? [To a student with hand raised] *Yes?*

Charles (C): Where did you get the 4 × 0?

Donna (D): [Calling out] *Oh, she's rounding off.*

T: When you multiplied 4 × 0 in the one's place, you made that a separate step?

J: Yes. Then I rounded off the 23 and I got 20.

T: Good.

Joan's method displayed a good understanding of place value, and it elicited mention of rounding off, which students had used in recent lessons to estimate answers to similar multiplication problems. Joan thought: 23 = 20 + 3. Then 20 + 3 = 2 tens and 0 ones + 3 more ones.

It is interesting that although Joan's method was very close to Patty's standard algorithm, she understood her own method and yet she may not have understood Patty's.

Let's go back to the fourth and final presenter in our example.

Teacher (T): Nick, yours puzzles me a little bit. Go ahead.

Nick (N): I had 4 × 25 = 100, and 100 − 8 = 92. And 25 wasn't the number; it was 23. So I had to take away 8 from the 100 and I got 92.

Nick rounded the 23 up to 25, multiplied 4 × 25, and then compensated for the rounding up by subtracting 4 2's. By mentioning her own (perhaps pretended, perhaps real) puzzlement, the teacher let the class know that she expected students to be puzzled by his method, and that puzzlement is an acceptable response in math class.

Anna (A): But how did you get the 8?

N: It was 23. 23 + 2 = 25. 25. And I had to take away 2 from all of them.

T: So, how did you count? Maybe that's the step we're missing.

N: I did it—I had two—so I did 2, 4, 6, 8.

T: 2, 4, 6, 8. All right. Any questions for Nick? [Pause] For anyone else? All right.

After all four strategies had been presented, Karen gave students one last chance to ask any presenter a question. Then she called for response from the whole class, to bring them back together and to give them a chance to participate with the presenters.

T: How many had the same method as Patty? As Ray? as Joan? as Nick? Look how many ways we did it! Let's give these four a hand!

Class: [Applauds with enthusiasm]

T: Thank you all. You may return to your seats.

Karen concluded the cluster interview by congratulating her students for their work and by eliciting applause, both to reward and to relax her class after their efforts.

As the class began, Karen had wished to know how well her class understood the distributive property, because she planned to teach them how it is used in two-digit multiplication. Notice that Patty, Ray, Joan, and Nick all used the distributive property in some way, without referring to it directly. None of them relied exclusively on other, more primitive methods such as simple repeated addition, tally counting, step-counting, or counting of groups of manipulative objects.

The distributive property says that when we wish to multiply A times B, we can get the answer by breaking A into parts, multiplying each of those parts by B, and adding the resulting products together. It generally is convenient to be able to break up numbers in this way. The distributive property allows us to find an infinite number of products without having to memorize an infinite number of multiplication facts.

Karen's students, wanting to multiply 4 times 23, found a variety of ways to break one of the numbers, either 23 or 4, into parts. Ray broke 4 into 3 plus 1 and multiplied each part times 23. The others all broke up the 23 and multiplied each of the parts by 4. Patty used the standard algorithm, which breaks 23 into 20 plus 3; Joan thought of 23 as 20 plus 0 plus 3; and Nick thinks of 23 as 25 plus a negative 2.

After asking, "How many had the same method as Patty? As Ray? as Joan? as Nick?" Karen now believed that most of her class was able to use the distributive property in multiplication. As a result, Karen predicted that her class would soon be able to use with understanding Patty's method—the standard algorithm for multiplication.

There are several advantages to Karen's interview cluster technique. Some advantages benefit the students at the blackboard. Students' self-esteem and self-image as innovative thinkers are enhanced. The teacher is careful to ensure that every child is selected from time to time.

Those students who might be uncomfortable standing alone at the board are less anxious in a small group. The reward of applause after their presentations is shared by the whole group, so the presentation does not degenerate into a popularity contest. In this class, students are not afraid to expose their ideas to their classmates. They want to work at the blackboard.

Notice that in Karen's class only correct solutions were represented at the board. Sometimes it is useful to invite a student to present an interesting but incorrect solution. Students should feel that it is a good idea to learn from mistakes.

A variety of solutions becomes a goal for everyone. Students understand that a diversity of approaches will be valued. Even a very primitive strategy may be selected, if it is not commonly shared. Not only the math whiz gets to go to the board. No matter how simple or how sophisticated the solution, the challenge of explaining it to the class is exciting. Putting one's thoughts into words that other students will understand is a valuable but not an easy experience. The teacher helps by asking leading questions, by clarifying statements made by the students, and by thinking aloud herself when she sees that help is needed.

Other advantages benefit the audience. First, students are exposed to a wide range of problem-solving strategies. A student who is not quite able to solve a problem unaided hears and sees alternatives, some of which may be immediately helpful.

Second, the side-by-side presentation of different solutions makes a strong visual impact. It is possible to compare and relate different solutions when they are displayed at the same time. Those who had no difficulty with the problem may still develop a richer, more integrated understanding of its various means of solution.

Finally, active audience participation in the questioning of presenters keeps the class interested and involved. The whole class enjoys this form of interviewing. The format is predictable, but the ideas are often surprising. Two or three clusters may be interviewed in this way during a single lesson.

What You Can Do

How can you use cluster interviews in your classroom to assess your students' understanding of mathematical concepts? Keep in your mind any questions that you have about your students. Select presenters with those questions in mind. Assess your class during the lesson. As you listen to their presentations, you will get information that will answer your questions.

First, make sure that students have something meaningful to share with their classmates. To avoid repetition, make sure that varied strategies are represented. You can control this by walking about the room as students write, inspecting their work. You may make either mental or written notes to aid you in your selection of interesting and varied strategies.

The selection of presenters is an important step. It gives you, the teacher, the opportunity to select strategies in a useful sequence and in interesting combinations. Perhaps the first group to go to the board will have more primitive methods, while a later group will present methods that are more sophisticated, or that build on those initial, primitive methods. Or perhaps each cluster will share common elements in their thinking strategies.

After selecting a useful mix of strategies, you invite to the board a cluster of three or four or five students, and give each student a clearly marked off space in which to write. At the board, mark sections off with vertical lines, giving students enough room to write side by side. Because they write their strategies all at the same time, there is little delay; meanwhile, the class is occupied in watching the different strategies unfold, line by line. Remind the presenters to turn and face the class to signal that they are finished writing. When all are ready, interview each student in turn and encourage the class to question them as well.

Each presenter should be asked at least one question. Because they indicate interest and respect, questions promote self-esteem as well as challenge. If the method seems to be understood by all and there are no student questions, you yourself may ask the presenter to justify, clarify, or extend the method presented.

When a teacher hopes to get students to invent an algorithm or procedure, it very often happens that one or more students already will have learned the standard algorithm from a parent or older friend or sibling. What do you do when you ask students for their own strategies yet a student presents the standard algorithm in a rote fashion? Such students often do not understand the algorithm well enough to explain why and how it works. This need not interfere with your plans, if you accept the algorithm as one of many strategies, without calling special attention to it.

An important aspect of this type of cluster interview is that your students are enabled to compare their own strategies with similar strategies presented by their friends, thereby better understanding both standard and alternative algorithms. Indeed, this comparison process may be spontaneous. You don't have to force it. You can allow your students to draw their own conclusions when they are ready to do so.

Another important aspect is that each presenter is the expert on his or her own method. You should refer all questions to the student expert, rather than attempting to provide explanations yourself. You are the moderator; you decide who speaks, but you do not answer questions yourself.

There is a fuzzy line between interpreting the expert's remarks and giving an explanation yourself. At times you may feel that you need to interpret what the expert says, as Karen did for Joan. But it is a good idea, whenever possible, to let the experts speak for themselves and to ask them to explain again when their classmates do not understand. In this way, you empower both them and their audience. After all, you are trying to teach them to articulate their thoughts. If you put words into their mouths, they are relieved of the important responsibility of finding the right words themselves.

How well do you have to understand the math you are teaching in order to successfully conduct cluster interviews? The deeper your mathematical knowledge, the better you can question students in a cluster interview. But you do not need to be able to invent everything the students do. Karen confided that she herself didn't always follow the reasoning behind every path her students took, but still she was willing to encourage them to share their methods. She did have a good understanding of the basic concepts of arithmetic and was always eager to learn more. That eagerness was evident to her students.

A deep understanding of basic concepts is a great advantage for the teacher who wants to use interviewing in this way, as it is for any teacher. As we have mentioned before, however, learning to interview is a long-term process. During that long-term process, cluster interviews foster in the teacher, as well as in the students, an ever-deepening sense of mathematics.

These are the steps Karen followed as she interviewed clusters of students. You may follow them as you interview clusters in your own classroom.

1. Assign a challenging written task involving a mathematical concept that underlies what you are trying to teach your students.

2. Observe students work as they write, noting which solutions are either of interest to your teaching goal or your assessment goal, or are unusual and interesting in their own right.

3. Select appropriate candidates for presentation at the board.

4. Mark off on the board a section for each presenter, using vertical lines.

5. Call on a group to go to the board, taking their written work with them.

6. Tell students to write their work at the board and to turn around and face the class when they are ready.

7. When all are ready and facing the class, ask the first on the left to present a strategy.

8. While a student is presenting, do not interrupt and do not permit students to interrupt.

9. Call on students who have questions for the "expert."

10. Ask a question yourself if you wish the expert to elaborate further or if no one else has asked a question.

11. Call on the other students, one at a time, and repeat steps 8, 9, and 10 for each one. Throughout, use this opportunity to assess the mathematical understanding of your students as individuals and as a group.

12. Give students a last chance to ask questions and bring the discussion to a close.

13. Praise the group for the diversity of their methods. Elicit applause from the class as students return to their seats.

Steps 5 through 13 may be repeated one or more times to give more students a chance in the limelight. Two or even three groups may fit into a half-hour lesson.

▲ *Interviewing During Whole-Class Instruction*

One of the teacher's major responsibilities is to help students bridge the gap between what they understand well and what they are only beginning to understand. This is where ongoing, informal assessment comes into the picture. When interviewing is a normal part of classroom procedure, when students' ideas are out in the open, the teacher is in a good position to know on a daily basis what students think and understand and therefore what instruction should follow next.

If you wish to integrate assessment and teaching successfully in a whole-class situation, you need to listen well and to know your students and your mathematics well. Fortunately, whole-class interviewing will offer you ample opportunities to improve your listening skills, your knowledge of students, and your knowledge of mathematics.

As was the case in our cluster interview example, whole-class interviewing elicits individual children's thoughts and strategies. This takes time. Before you object that you will never be able to get through all the problems you hoped to use in your lesson, consider selecting one, two, or a very few representative problems that will be studied in depth. This "less is more" approach will help your students learn from discussion with their peers and will reveal to you their individual strengths and weaknesses. Extended discussion of a very few examples, in contrast to rapid coverage of many examples, is a teaching strategy that is common in successful Japanese classrooms (Stevenson & Stigler, 1992).

You will be able to use one student's misconceptions to explore areas that may be difficult for many. You will find that your students' creative thoughts give you new ideas. Your own teaching strategies will be refreshed by examples from your students' work.

As students' thinking is awarded the place of honor in your classroom, you will find that both you and your students are making more connections between their individual strategies—connections that deepen mathematical understanding.

How can you facilitate the making of such connections? To see how all this might work in practice, let us look at an example.

What Diana Did

Diana, a second-grade teacher, does a good job of integrating teaching and assessment. In her classroom, students' ideas have center stage. In our example, her class was already comfortable with simple subtraction and they were just beginning to learn subtraction with borrowing. Before she asked her students to work independently with pencil and paper, Diana planned to help them to understand the need for regrouping and borrowing. Together they would explore several ways to find answers to problems. Later they would work with pencil and paper.

In keeping with a "less is more" philosophy, the entire discussion was devoted to a single problem. Diana called on one student after another, encouraging them to share their strategies for solving that problem.

Here, then, is a description of the entire lesson. The class began as the students were seated on the floor close to the board, grouped about Diana, who stood at the board.

> **Teacher (T):** *Here's the problem. We have 45 things to start out with and we're going to take 29 of them away. Walt, don't give us the answer. Can you represent that for us on the board?*
>
> **Walt (W):** *Which way shall I write it?*
>
> **T:** *Either way. It's interesting that you know that there are two ways.*
>
> **W:** [Writes the problem horizontally.]
>
> **T:** *Is there another way you could represent this?*
>
> **W:** *Yes.*
>
> **T:** *Could you write that one?*
>
> **W:** [Writes the problem vertically.]
>
> **T:** *Now, whether we write it this way* [Pointing]*, which is horizontally, whether we write it this way, which is vertically, are we going to get different answers, each time we do it?*
>
> **Students:** *No!*

Notice that Diana reminded her students right at the beginning of the lesson that mathematics is more than just getting an answer. She wants her students to believe that the answer comes as a result of thinking.

Diana began by stating the problem aloud, demonstrating that the problem is independent of the written algorithm. Her students knew that very well: they often practiced mental math. Notice, too, that she gave her students an opportunity to affirm that the method of representation does not affect the answer to the problem. This important mathematical idea had been learned in prior lessons. Here it was reviewed, made explicit, and incorporated into the current lesson. Whole-class interviews, because they do not rush through too much material, provide many such opportunities along the way to review and incorporate students' prior knowledge.

Diana used a large mathematical vocabulary with her class. Her students came to understand such words as *vertically*, *horizontally*, and *represent* by hearing them in context. When heard often in context, even these sophisticated words are easily learned.

Now let us see how Diana encouraged her first volunteer. She suggested that each student would have a "way" to figure out the answer, and that she was interested in each of those ways.

> *Teacher (T): Is this an easy problem? Can you just look at it and easily say the answer? No. So there are ways to figure out the answer, and I want to know Jennifer's way.*
>
> *T: [To Jennifer] Go ahead. Try it. How would you do it?*
>
> *Jennifer (J): [After some thought] Counting down.*
>
> *T: Counting down. Good.*
>
> *J: 45, 44, 43, oopsie! [Pauses as she loses track.]*

Jennifer's method of subtraction was not a sophisticated one. She still was counting down, as were other students in her class, when she was unable to find the answer in any other way. Yet Diana respected her choice and urged her to continue.

Sometimes, however, a student's plan goes awry. Counting down from 45 to 29 was not easy for Jennifer, especially in front of the class. She began to lose track. Let's see how Diana managed to rescue Jennifer.

> *T: Is it hard to count down with such large numbers? Do you want some time to do it, and then get back to us?*
>
> *J: Yes.*
>
> *T: O.K. I'm going to give you some privacy. I'm going to let you go outside in the hall where it's real quiet, count down, and then come back in and report to us what you think it is.*
>
> *J: Can I take the blocks?*
>
> *T: Absolutely. Absolutely. You may take anything you need.*

Jennifer was clearly relieved to be able to go out in the hall to count with the blocks. While Jennifer was out of the room, the teacher called for another strategy.

Teacher (T): *Who has a strategy that's different from counting down? Gary?*

Gary (G): [Confidently, starting from the left and subtracting the smaller number from the larger in each column] *Well, I know that this column is 40 and this column is the ones. So I'll take 20 away from 40. I know that if I take 2 away from 4 that leaves 2, so if I take 20 away from 40 that leaves 20. So I'll put a 2 here. Then all I have to do is subtract the ones. I know that 10 minus 5 is 5 and so 9 minus 5 is 4 and so I put a 4 here.*

T: *Whoa, whoa, whoa. You said that 10 minus 5 is 5 and that's a 9 so that's 1 less.*

G: *So that will have to be 1 less.*

T: *Is it asking you to take 5 away from 9 or is it saying that you have to take 9 away from 5?*

G: *It is saying I have to take 5 away from 9.*

T: [In a doubting tone] *Is it really?*

Students: *No.*

T: *They don't agree with you. They say you're not taking 5 away from 9 because you have 5 up here and this 9 down here* [Pointing] *tells you what you have to take away.*
[A hum of excited conversation follows. This is a key issue and several students are confused about it.]
If you take 9 away from 5 what do you get?

Student: *– 4.*

T: *You're saying you have negative numbers now.*

When a subtraction example requires one to subtract a larger digit from a smaller one, students respond in many ways. Some, like Gary, are not ready to give up the familiar, mechanical one-column-at-a-time method, which they learned with numbers that do not require borrowing. Some count down and thus avoid the issue entirely. Some know that subtraction is not commutative: 9 – 5 is not the same as 5 – 9.

It may seem unusual that some in this second-grade class even know about the existence of numbers that are less than zero. Diana later explained that her student's father had told him at home about negative numbers. You may wonder why Diana called attention to that student's comment by remarking, "You're saying you have negative numbers now." Surely she was not attempting to teach her class about that topic. But Diana's policy is to accept all of her students' ideas. Just as she accepts primitive strategies, she also accepts sophisticated ones, weaving them all into the discussion and involving her students in mathematical thinking.

Notice that this teacher encouraged the class to call out. In fact, calling out kept her students actively involved. She remained in control, however; when a student had been called on to speak, all others were required to remain silent and to listen. This teacher turned the vocal participation off and on with a sweep of the hand, somewhat like the gesture of an orchestra conductor.

You are the one in charge in your classroom, and Diana's style may not be the one you yourself prefer to use. You may find other ways to encourage all students to participate and to listen to one another. Matters of discipline and order may be decided on the basis of their impact on your vision of the thinking classroom. There are many ways to make that vision a reality.

Diana took advantage of students' voices to show Gary that his way was not acceptable to some of the class. Some teachers might feel that this appeal to the students unfairly exposed Gary to their negative response. Diana felt that it was important for Gary to know that his strategy was not working, and she preferred to let him hear that message from his peers, who were also actively engaged in thinking about the problem. In this situation, Gary's confidence, abundant at the start, did not seem to be diminished at all.

We will see later that when Gary gets into a strategy that confuses even his teacher, she does ask him to sit down to listen to a variety of other strategies; she hopes that his peers will help him understand that which she herself is at present unable to help him with.

But let's go back to our example. Notice throughout that although Gary has a voice that is loud and clear as well as incorrect, Diana continues to reflect his statements both aloud and in writing, so that each student in the class is aware of what he has said.

Now that the class had shown that some of them saw more to the problem than Gary had seen, she began to try to help him specifically, and those like him as well.

> *T:* [To Gary] *Let me ask you this. I've got 5 fingers here, Gary. Can you take 9 of them away?*
>
> *G: You can take 5 of them away.*
>
> *T: You can take 5 of them away, and then when 5 of them are used up then you have to go and get somebody else's somewhere.*

G: *You have to regroup.*

T: *You have to regroup. Good. So if you're going to regroup, how do you do that?*

To help Gary modify his thinking, the teacher went back to a concrete example, fingers. The fingers and the phrase "go and get somebody else's" reminded Gary that he had heard before about this difficulty, and he remembered that such situations call for something called "regrouping." The teacher was not satisfied with the word alone. She wanted to know what Gary meant by it.

G: *I get 35.*

T: *You think it's 35.* [She writes 35 under the problem.] *Tell me how you got 35.*

G: *First I thought you had to put it down but then it wasn't right so instead of putting it down I took the 4 and I put it up here* [pointing as he speaks]. *Then I took the 1 that was still left and I put it onto the 3 and I get 35.*

T: *Do you agree with him, Michael?*

Michael (M): *No.*

T: *Michael doesn't agree with you, Gary. Let's see what Jennifer will say. This is a time to think.*

Gary had made a very common subtraction error. He began at the left, in the tens column. Then in the ones column he subtracted the smaller digit from the larger. Gary was confident and articulate, but his facility with words did not prevent him from making that common mistake. He knew that the 2 and 4 in the tens column stood for 20 and 40. He knew how to use one fact, $10 - 5 = 5$ to get another neighboring fact, $9 - 5 = 4$. But he didn't relate the tens digit to the ones digit in either of the numbers.

This mini-interview showed the teacher exactly how Gary thought about the problem. Next, she tried to get him to question the correctness of his thinking.

Gary seemed only a little less confident as he explained his version of borrowing. The teacher was rather confused by Gary's way of arriving at an answer, which seemed to involve carrying. Again, she used student disagreement to challenge Gary's method. She wished to encourage her students to question one another as well as themselves.

This time she did not tell Gary that he was wrong. Instead, she reminded the class that Jennifer would soon return to contribute to the discussion. She asked them to think and to weigh all the evidence before making any decision about the solution to the problem.

Diana allowed Gary to sit down and asked Kai to use an estimation strategy.

> *Teacher (T): Kai, what number is 29 very close to?*
>
> *Kai (K): 30.*
>
> *T: What if you take 30 away from 45?*
>
> *Students:* [Calling out] *I know the answer, you get 25. 15. So the answer is 14. No, 16. I think it's 18.*
>
> *K: Well, I know that 45 take away 30 is 15. But 29 is one less so I had to put one more on and so I put 16.*
>
> *T:* [Who has listed on the board each answer suggested] *Thank you. Notice we've got a range here. No one has said 100.*

Diana had wanted to see whether estimation would help her students understand the problem better. Kai was able to use rounding to come to an accurate answer, but many other students offered a range of guesses. Diana took advantage of this guessing to list all of their guesses on the board. She noted that the guesses were not far off the mark. In this way she kept the interest of seated students and encouraged them not to give up. By calling attention to the narrow range within which the answers fell, she implied that students would find a reasonable answer to the problem. She wanted her students to feel that math makes sense.

All this while, Jennifer had been counting blocks. Now she returned triumphantly.

> *T: Jennifer's back. She has something to report to us. Jennifer, what did you find out by counting down?*
>
> *Jennifer (J): 16.*
>
> *T: So Jennifer counting down found out that it was 16. Thank you, Jennifer.*

As Jennifer announced her answer, the teacher drew a star on the board opposite the 16 on the list of possible answers. Still, the class had come to no definitive conclusion about the answer to their problem.

T: Let's hear from some other people. Douglas, we haven't heard from you.

Douglas (D): [Going to the board and pointing] *If this was a 9 we would have 1 less.*

T: So what would you get?

D: 16.

T: So you're with Jennifer.

Chorus of students: *I'll go with Jennifer.*

When Douglas said, "If this was a 9 we would have 1 less," he meant 1 less to take away. His shorthand explanation was understood and accepted by the teacher. The students were swayed by his validation of Jessica's answer. Diana might have asked him to explain his strategy a bit further to the class, but her attention was diverted by a visual distraction created by another student.

T: [In a new and very serious tone] I'm going to have Pat either join us or he can go out. This is very disturbing . . . Rosa, remember what I said?

Although much commotion may be permitted when it is directly related to the math work, it is wise not to let irrelevant distraction go very far. In our example, Diana put a stop to it quickly, gave Rosa a stern look for good measure, and returned to the flow of the discussion.

Anna next raised her hand to offer a strategy. Her offer was accepted, for Diana knew that Anna was able to use the standard subtraction algorithm with regrouping, or borrowing.

T: Anna, what is your strategy?

Anna (A): [Calculates the answer at the board, correctly using the standard subtraction algorithm with borrowing.] *I took one from this 4.*

T: [Disapprovingly] So you took 1 from this 4?

A: 10.

T: O.K., so you took 10. What did you do with that 10?

A: I put it up next to the 5.

T: So you have 10 and 5 more, and that makes 15. O.K., so that's why you put that there.

A: Then I took 9 from the 15 and I put 6. Then I took 2 from the 3 . . .

T: From the 3?

A: 30. Then 30 take away 20 equals 10.

T: So what's your conclusion?

A: 16.

T: O.K., so you're agreeing with Jennifer and Douglas.

Diana had hoped to show the class that a variety of strategies led successfully to the same answer. First inviting primitive counting down strategies, and gradually eliciting more sophisticated strategies involving estimation and working from the nearest ten, she ended with a student who understood regrouping. Diana insisted that Anna not only perform the algorithm correctly but also explain it using terminology that referred to the place value of each digit. In this way, she hoped to take some of the mystery out of the procedure and enable students to relate it to their other strategies.

T: Did anyone else use the same strategy that Anna used? [Pointing to upraised hands] *You did, you did, you did, you did . . .*

Student: I have a different strategy.

T: No, I want to know who used the same *strategy. You did, you did, you did . . .*

Diana now had a rough idea of the number of students who were beginning to understand Anna's method. This gave her an idea about how to proceed in the next day's lesson. It also gave students an opportunity to assess themselves.

T: Which are easier—are adding problems easier, or are subtraction problems easier?

Students: Adding.

A student: I like both.

T: You like both! What were we doing in these problems today?

Students: Take away.

T: Take away. What's another name for take away?

Students: Subtraction.

T: Subtraction. And what did I tell you you had invented yesterday?

Students: Regrouping! Borrowing!

T: Regrouping with borrowing. Good. O.K. We're going to do a little more of that. You're doing it in your head and at the board. But soon we'll begin to see how you can do it with pencil and paper.

In the course of the lesson, Diana learned much about her students' understanding of subtraction with regrouping. Her students learned to articulate their thoughts and to listen to one another. As they responded to the variety of strategies presented by their peers, they deepened their understanding of important mathematical concepts.

What You Can Do

How do you manage this kind of lesson? How do you get your students to listen well and to respond to one another's ideas? Here are some additional pointers to help you get started.

Unless your students are writing, you may wish to arrange to have your class sit up close to you, even on the floor, for math lessons. Your students will concentrate better when they are separated from distracting materials at their seats. In this way you can maintain control over them and observe and listen to them well. Most important, they can listen well to one another.

After the problem is presented and procedures are established, you will begin to elicit strategies from individual students. You will want them to be willing to try what, for them, may be a difficult problem. If you let your students know that you respect their best efforts, they will be willing to share those efforts with the class. Your students pick up your attitudes from your voice, your words, your actions, and your gestures. Model respect and your students will learn to respect one another.

Try to keep all of your students involved. Make sure they can all hear one another. Insist on silence from the class when a student has been called on to speak. You may wish to reflect back to the class what a student has said, to make sure that everyone has heard it or to emphasize an important point. You can do this both by repeating the student's words aloud and by writing them on the blackboard or on a flipchart so that all students are able to read them. In either case, use the students' words whenever you can. A good way to show that you respect a student is to respect that student's words. If you validate students' words in this way, they will feel that you respect what they have said and will be willing to share their thoughts again.

Model connection-making yourself as you refer back often to students' ideas by name. For example, you might say, "Your method is very much like Jaimie's" or "How many of you did it Sandra's way?" or "Tom and Debra have different answers. Can they both be right?"

Whether successful every time or not, if you encourage your students to use their strategies in their chosen ways, you give them a sense of purpose and self-esteem. Students who know that their thinking is respected and accepted develop confidence. That confidence facilitates a willingness to share their thoughts. You can develop it in your students if you accept their work, their effort, and their strategies, even when they do not always lead to success.

Do not be afraid to allow students to present erroneous thinking. Your students will not learn the wrong way just because they have heard or seen it. In fact, errors expressed, brought to light, and explored are more likely to be corrected than those that are suppressed. Whenever one student presents an error, there are probably others who share that erroneous thinking. If sharing and discussion help clarify a concept for the presenter, they may also help those others to correct their own thinking.

What should you do when a student at the board becomes frustrated or unable to proceed? You wish the student to succeed, but you see that immediate success is not likely. How can you provide a rescue? Offer the student some time to think about the problem while others share their ideas. Offer a second chance to speak later on if it becomes apparent that suggestions from peers have brought about a new understanding.

When one strategy becomes obviously unproductive, it is a good idea to switch to a new strategy. In this way you model for your students your belief that there are many ways to arrive at an answer, and when one way does not work, another way may be more productive. When calling on another student, you may wish to suggest a new approach quite explicitly, as Diana did.

If there is any one major hurdle for teachers who want to use interviewing in the classroom, it is right here in this process and product issue. If you are interested in getting your students to talk about how they think about a problem, you will wish to let them know that you are not interested only, or even mainly, in the answer. You are interested primarily in their thinking process. Later, when their understanding is better consolidated and subtraction with borrowing, for example, is no longer difficult for them, then your students may concern themselves with accuracy and speed.

When your class begins to tire, or the scheduled time is near its end, you must bring closure to the discussion. Because the discussion is about students' thinking, and that thinking process may not be complete, the discussion often will have to be continued another day. Still, you wish to end the lesson by giving your students a sense of accomplishment.

When you know your students well, you can sometimes select a student who will be able to wrap up the discussion for you. If this is not the case, it is up to you to review what has been accomplished and indicate how the discussion will be continued at a future time.

As you conclude a whole-class interview, it is a good idea to give all of your students a final chance for active participation. A show of hands is simple and quick, but it serves the purpose. It may also provide you with assessment information. A show of hands with rapid-fire questioning involves even more active participation than a simple show of hands. It allows you to review the lesson with the class and leave them excited and eager for the next one. Diana used this technique at the very end of her lesson.

Finally, don't forget to celebrate a successful lesson and to congratulate all the participants. They will have been working hard at a difficult but rewarding job.

Every teacher develops a unique teaching style. The guidelines that follow are not offered as a model to copy. They represent only one of many ways to incorporate interviewing into the classroom. You will be able to think of many variations of the whole-class interview as you combine or alternate it in different ways with individual written work, with small-group instruction, and with cooperative group work. The strength of the whole-class interview is that it encourages students to learn in collaboration with their peers. Here, then, are some suggested guidelines.

1. Present the problem to the class.
2. Establish your expectations from the start. Let the class know that they will share strategies first. The answer will come only later.
3. Let the students know from the start that you expect them to be involved in the discussion.
4. Let students know that although they will be asked to do something that may be difficult, you expect them to be able to do it.
5. Call to mind previously learned vocabulary and concepts that are related to this lesson.

6. Remind students that there will be many acceptable ways to solve the problem.

7. Call on a student to share a strategy.

8. Allow each student to be in control of his or her own strategy for solving the problem.

9. Don't be afraid to confront conceptual difficulties as they arise. They may represent the heart of the problem at hand.

10. Keep the class involved in those difficult issues by calling for and responding to their participation.

11. If a student needs help, provide no more help than is needed.

12. If progress comes to a dead end, ask students to reflect on what has been accomplished so far and suggest that the class look for a different approach to the problem.

13. Summarize the progress made by the class so far. Point to the fact that the range of possible answers has been narrowed down.

14. Repeat steps 7 through 13 as often as you think is right.

15. Give the entire class a final chance to register their involvement.

16. Congratulate the class for a job well done.

▲ What Comes Next?

In the next chapter, we will explore examples of another exciting form of interviewing—peer interviewing—in which children learn to interview one another.

CHAPTER FIVE

▲ *Peer Interviewing*

In the "thinking classroom," it is not only teachers who want to learn what students think. Students enjoy sharing their thinking among themselves as well. Perhaps you would like to take a giant step beyond the ideas described in preceding chapters. Perhaps you would like to teach your students to interview one another. Teachers in our project did just that.

In this chapter we will see how teachers worked with their students to help them do two things:

- Develop an understanding of the interview.
- Develop the skills necessary to interview each other.

Teaching children to interview one another is useful for them in many ways. In our work we observed that children can learn from peers as a result of interviewing each other. They learn about each other's thinking, they learn about the content of the interview, and they learn how to express their feelings. They may even find that their peers' feelings are much like their own.

Children are more secure and self-confident when they know that others share similar feelings. One teacher described the effects of students' sharing with peers when she reported:

Peer questioning made it less threatening for the students [than when I questioned them]. I saw the progress in my students. I feel the kids who had trouble in math are doing better and most of the questioning comes from them. One student who was so isolated is now beginning to ask questions. Another one was very shaky in math, afraid to verbalize, and now is asking questions. Another girl is asking questions as well. Before, she wouldn't have. She has the nerve now to get up and do it.

Other goals are accomplished when children learn to interview each other. Children learn to know better what is expected of them. They begin to value their thinking and that of others. No longer concerned exclusively with getting the right answer to a problem, they begin to shift the focus of their efforts to finding a strategy to solve it.

Peer interviews provide some additional advantages that are provided by flexible interviews in general. The peer interview makes children's thinking much more overt; it brings to light events that might otherwise pass unnoticed. It brings more of the cognitive processes out into the open where teachers and students can examine and try to understand them.

What follows is a detailed review of how one teacher has trained children in the skill of interviewing. Through excerpts of classroom interviews, we will illustrate the work of Susan, a combined first and second grade teacher at a Public School in New York City. The focus of Susan's work is problem-solving. Her students learn to interview one another about how they work to solve problems.

▲ *Introducing Interviewing in the Classroom*

The first step in teaching children how to interview each other is to get them to understand the goal of the flexible interview. Young children are not familiar with flexible interviewing. Perhaps they have never before been interviewed. Most probably they have never conducted an interview themselves. They need to learn that the goal of interviewing is to develop an understanding of someone else's thinking, and that to achieve that goal, the interviewer uses open-ended questions.

Now, let's see how Susan began.

What Susan Did

To introduce interviewing in her classroom, Susan gave her students pretend questions.

> *Teacher (T): In an interview, if somebody says, "Let me see how you got your answer," what are you going to do?*
>
> *Peter (P): Show them the way that you did it.*
>
> *T: Show them the way that you did it, from beginning to end.*

Next, Susan gave her students a pretend question and created a discussion around it. With the pretend question she focused children's thinking on a concrete situation.

> *T: If George just asked, "Can you show me your answer?" is it the same as saying, "Can you show me how you got your answer?"*
>
> **Sara (S): *No.***
>
> *T: Why not?*
>
> *S: Because it is shorter, and it doesn't show how you got your answer. It is like from the "end," and how you got it, not like how you did it. That will be from beginning to end.*

Notice that Susan asked her students to compare two different but very similar questions. That comparison was quite important. It made students begin to think about the goal of the interview and the importance of questioning. What is it that the interviewer is looking for? The question that you ask can really make a difference in the answer that you get.

Let's see how Susan tried to get her students to think about the importance of process as well as of product.

> *T: Do you think it is important to see the beginning and the end?*
>
> **Donald (D): *No.***
>
> *T: Wait a minute. If you want to understand how somebody figured something out, is it important to see the process from the beginning to end?*
>
> *D: No.*
>
> *T: You don't think you need to?*
>
> *D: No, because the part that really counts is the end, because that's the answer.*

We see that Donald gives more importance to the product than to the process. Donald will have a difficult time interviewing someone if he does not learn to value the process as well as the product.

With her last two questions, Susan seemed to have been pressuring Donald to look at the interview from a different perspective. Susan's pressure did not affect Donald's answer. Let's see how the dialogue continued.

T: What is the point of the interview? The interview is not to say what was the answer. The point of the interview is . . . what? Why are you interviewing somebody?

Robert (R): *To see how they did it.*

T: So, is just showing your answer, the end, going to tell you how they did it?

Note that Susan worked with her students, trying to get them to think about the goal of the interview. Through this approach, she was able to get her students to develop an understanding of the goal of the interview without having to tell them explicitly what it is. There is an advantage to her approach. Students are thinking and constructing their own understanding of the goal of the interview. When people construct their own learning rather than simply being told about the concept or skill, they are more likely to make the concept or skill their own.

What You Can Do

Your goal is to get your students to understand the purpose of interviewing and how to use questions to accomplish this goal. There are different ways to introduce the concept of interviewing in the classroom. You may begin by asking your students to tell you what they know about its purpose. Give pretend questions and/or present concrete examples of questions and situations that may occur in an interview. It is easier for young children to relate to concrete situations which give them a clear picture of what they are being asked to discuss. Using pretend questions facilitates the discussion with younger students.

Or you can conduct discussions about interviewing by beginning with the abstract question, "What is a flexible interview?" Abstract questions probably would be more appropriate with older students.

Some teachers may begin by simply telling their students what the flexible interview is all about. In fact, giving students a lecture about a topic is an alternative considered by many teachers. But when the goal is to develop understanding, lecturing may not be the most productive option. Perhaps the lecture may best be used as a brief introduction to the topic, in the manner of an organizer.

Traditionally, the product, or the right answer quickly given, has been all that mattered. Children are in the habit of valuing mainly the product or the answer. But in conducting a flexible interview, children need to value process and understanding. When students discuss the nature of questioning, they begin to get an idea of the importance of process in the tasks that they engage in. If these issues are discussed in advance in the classroom, before engaging in the task of interviewing, students will begin to conduct interviews that assess process, rather than product.

If you want to get your students to value process as well as product, be aware that their beliefs, values, and attitudes have direct impact on their capacity to change. If students' beliefs, attitudes, and values are in disagreement with the type of teaching and learning that you wish to foster in your classroom, there will be little collaboration and little change. Therefore, in order to develop your students' understanding of the interview, question your students about how they value both process and product. For this purpose, a teacher may wish to ask questions like these: "Is just showing your answer going to tell other people how you did it?" "How is your method of solving the problem different from the answer you get?"

To review, in order to develop students' understanding of the concept of flexible interviewing, follow these steps:

1. Use guided discussions and questions to get your students to think about the goal of the interview.
2. Use concrete situations and/or pretend questions as much as possible.
3. Encourage your students to reflect about the role of process and of product in interviewing.
4. Question your students' values, feelings, and attitudes about both process and product.

▲ *Using Role Reversal to Teach Interviewing*

Role reversal is a technique often used to teach skills. In role reversal, teacher and students exchange roles. The teachers we worked with used role reversal to teach students how to interview one another. The teacher became the interviewee and the student became the interviewer.

In using role reversal, teachers found it helpful to do the following:

- Answer their students' questions incompletely in order to challenge them to ask better questions.
- Teach students to create questions that would help interviewees become aware of and able to speak about their thinking strategies.

There are several advantages to using role reversal. Because students are given the opportunity to play the roles they will be engaged in later on, they can begin to anticipate what is expected of them, both as interviewers and as interviewees. And student role playing allows the teacher to provide coaching and support as the student develops interviewing skills.

Let us continue to look at how Susan taught her students. Her work will give you some ideas about how to use role reversal to teach your students how to interview each other.

What Susan Did

Susan began by presenting a simple word problem and asking her students to interview her about how she solved it.

> *Teacher (T): You are going to watch and you are going to help Sara interview me about a simple problem. I am going to give you a simple problem. O.K., this is the problem: "There were 3 fish swimming in the ocean, a big shark came along and ate up 2. How many were left?" Shh . . . all right, so I figured it out. [Children raise their hands to give the answer to the problem.] No. Listen, we are not doing answers. Listen to me. Listen, listen. I figured out my answer. Now, Sara, come over to me to interview me and ask me how I figured out my answer. O.K.?*

Notice how difficult it was for students to wait for the interview to take place. They all wanted to give the answer to the problem, since that is what they were used to doing. Yet Susan kept to the task, giving students clear and direct instructions about what they were expected to do.

Let's see how Sara interviewed Susan, her teacher.

> *Sara (S): How did you figure out your answer? Did you do it like everybody else, or did you use your thoughts and do it very uniquely?*
>
> *T: Well, I just kind of thought it up in my head.*

S: It is not complete.

T: Well, I just kind of thought of it. I just thought that there were 3 fish and the shark came along and ate up 2 and I just thought of the answer. [Sara looked puzzled, not knowing what to say, but indicating with her look that she was not convinced her teacher was telling her what she was thinking.]

S: It is not complete.

T: Wait a minute, am I giving good answers to Sara? What is the problem here?

Notice that Susan gave incomplete and vague answers to Sara. In this way she tried to force Sara to develop better questions—questions that would help an interviewee to speak about her thoughts.

When Sara appeared puzzled, Susan resumed her role as a teacher and tried to involve the rest of the class. Her intervention may have prevented Sara from feeling frustrated. Perhaps the level of inquiry that Susan was promoting was far beyond Sara's skills. Let's see how Susan involved the rest of the class in the interview. She asked them to describe what she should have said.

Georgia (G): Well, there were 3 fish swimming in the ocean, and I used Unifix cubes, and I just took 2 away from the 3.

T: Oh, so I should actually tell her how I used the cubes? Did you see the cubes in front of me? Oh, you think that could be a better answer? Should I try that? I am going to try Georgia's suggestion, of saying exactly how I used the material. All right, well, I took three Unifix cubes to be the fish. So, these were the fish and then I figured a shark came along and I took 2 away. I put 2 over here. So, that's how I did it. Am I leaving anything out?

Notice how Susan went back and forth between the role of the actual teacher and the role of the interviewee. In this way she kept control of the task at the same time that she pressed students to think about producing good questions.

Sara (S): I don't think that's enough, because see, you are just saying, "Well, the shark came along and took 2 away" and you are supposed to say how you figured out that the shark took the 2 away and how many were left. Not just going to say, "Well, it took 2 away . . . "

T: So, I am not telling you enough?

S: No.

T: Who has a good interview question for me, to get me to explain what I did? Just pretend I am another kid and you had to interview me and I said, "Well, I don't know, so I just figured that the answer was 1."

S: Well, that's not really enough.

T: That's not really enough. What else would you want to know?

Peter (P): *How you figured it out.*

T: O.K., that's a good point. You want me to tell you how I figured it out. O.K. Can anybody think of a question to ask me, to get me to tell you what I did better?

Michael (M): *How do you know it is 1? It might be 2.*

T: Oh, good question: "How do I know?" Michael is asking me to prove it by showing it to him. You are asking me to prove it to you, using the cubes. Wasn't that an excellent question? Very good.

Notice how Susan engaged several students in the process of creating interview questions. It was not easy for them to come up with the questions. Yet, she was able to keep her students focused on the issue of questioning until they found a question that led to a more complete description of the strategies used.

What You Can Do

Role reversal is an effective way for you to give your students immediate corrective feedback as they practice interviewing.

Students who already are familiar with flexible interviews in the classroom are going to role-play an interview more easily than those who never have participated in an interview before. If your students are not familiar with flexible interviewing, review the guidelines in Chapter 2 about preparing students for flexible interviewing.

You may want to model first for your students the way in which you plan an interview in advance. Show your students how the plan helps set a goal and helps, too, in the selection of productive questions. You can model for your students how you carry out that plan in an interview. Finally, by thinking aloud, model how you monitor the original plan during the course of the interview. As you conduct the interview, show them how you assess the plan, make changes to it, and adapt it to the responses of the interviewee.

After you have modeled for your students how to plan, conduct, and monitor a flexible interview, you can have them conduct interviews in which they exchange roles with you. When students begin to practice interviewing through role reversal, you often will need to engage several of them in the process of questioning, because one child alone may not have the skill to carry out the entire interview. As soon as children are ready, however, give them the opportunity to carry out a complete interview. Experiencing the entire process gives them the "big picture" and a clear sense of what is expected of them.

While using role reversal, resume your role as a teacher whenever your students need someone to guide them.

To review, when using role reversal, follow these steps:

1. Begin by presenting a simple word problem.

2. Model how you plan an interview.

3. Model how you monitor the questions and the plan as you conduct the interview.

4. Model how you make changes to the plan as you carry it out.

5. Ask your students to engage in role reversal—that is, to interview you about how you solved the problem.

6. Set clear limits and instructions as to how you want them to conduct the interview.

7. Give incomplete and vague responses to your students, trying to force them to develop questions that help you speak about your thinking.

8. Go back and forth between the role of the teacher and the role of the interviewee as often as is necessary, to make sure that students participate in the way that is most productive.

9. As needed, engage several students in the process of creating interview questions.

▲ Brainstorming Interview Questions

Asking students to brainstorm interview questions is another way to teach children how to interview each other. When using this technique, teachers ask students to think of all the possible questions they might ask in relationship to a given task. Teachers who used this brainstorming technique found it helpful to do the following:

- Play the role of interviewee and ask students to suggest questions that they might wish to ask.
- Involve students in a discussion of the questions they have suggested.

Teachers who use this brainstorming technique do not tell their students what questions to ask. Instead, as they play the role of interviewee, their responses elicit questions from their students and give their students an opportunity to practice questioning techniques.

Next, let's take a look at how Susan had her students brainstorm interview questions.

What Susan Did

Susan had given her students a word problem to solve individually. Before interviewing one another about their strategies, the children brainstormed some useful questions. We will read next an illustration of what Susan did to elicit interview questions from her students.

> *T: Today I am going to hand you your sheets of paper. You'll pair up with somebody and you'll interview that person about their strategy. Now, one thing before we go. We talked last time about how sometimes it is hard to get people to really talk about how they came up with the answer. Remind me and remind each other about some good questions that might help somebody really tell you what they are thinking.*
>
> *Sara (S): What material?*
>
> *T: That's a good question. So, if you are going to interview somebody who used Unifix cubes, you would ask why they used that material. What would that tell you about that person?*

Notice Susan's intervention. Her last question, "What would that tell you about that person?" is a real thinking question. Sara's answer would let Susan know what her real intentions were when she posed the question about the materials. It would tell her if Sara was in fact thinking about assessing someone else's thinking, or if she was just posing a question by imitation. Let's see how Sara responded.

Sara (S): Ah . . . (Looking up at the ceiling)

Peter (P): The answer is not up there.

S: Why do you like using that material?

T: O.K., Why do you like using certain material? O.K.

Pat (P): Maybe you could ask them why you used it. I mean, I mean . . . how you used it.

T: Oh, how. To actually show you or tell you?

P: Show you.

T: Show you, O.K. What's another good question?

From the dialogue one might think that Sara probably had not thought much about the question before she posed it. Her eyes wandered up to the ceiling, and she took some time to answer. Yet, Susan's question did force Sara to think. Susan uses questions in the classroom not only as a tool to assess thinking, but also as a tool to foster it.

Let's see next how Susan continued to encourage her students to produce interview questions.

T: What's another good question to ask? What about if a person says, "I don't know, I just did it."

Robert (R): Tell them to prove it.

T: Prove it. Prove it to me. Good. If somebody tells you, "Prove it," you really have to show them how you did it, right?

R: Right, because they may say I did it like this and it might be another way.

Once again, we see how Susan encouraged her students to reflect on the purpose behind each question. This is the essence of the art of interviewing. The interviewer asks questions to explore a hypothesis—to learn something about the interviewee.

T: All right. How about if somebody says, we talked about this last time, "Well, I don't know, I just did it in my head. I just did it in my head."

John (J): You could ask, "What did you use in your head?"

T: O.K. "What did you use in your head?" What do you mean by that? "What did you use in your head?"

J: You could have used Unifix cubes, but in your head. You could have used sticks in your head. You could have used chalk in your head.

T: So, you mean pictures in your head?

J: Yes. You could have used . . .

T: Good. So you are actually asking the person what kind of picture they had in their brain when they were trying to figure out the answer.

In this segment, we saw how Susan listened very carefully to her students' thoughts. She was modeling for them how important it is to listen to another person, to pay close attention to what is being said, to paraphrase or mirror what was said, and to provide the necessary support for the one who expresses his or her thinking.

What You Can Do

Before students brainstorm interview questions, it is very important that you model for them how you, yourself, plan the questions for an interview. Make your students aware that interview questions are not just asked for the sake of asking them. Let them see that underlying each question there is a goal and/or a hypothesis to investigate.

Once you have modeled how you plan the interview questions, engage your students in brainstorming questions themselves. Get your students to reflect upon the goals and hypotheses that underlie their questions. To do this, ask them: "Why would you ask that question?" "What would you learn by asking that question?" "How do you know that your question will get him or her to talk about his or her thinking?" If you make your students think about their questions in this way, you are basically guiding them to plan and analyze their questions.

While you are asking your students to brainstorm questions, try to make them aware that the point is not just to ask any question. Good questions force the interviewee to think and speak about his or her thinking. These are questions such as, "Why did you choose that strategy?" or "How did you use the strategy?"

As you work with your students, model careful listening. Help them to become aware of how carefully you listen to their questions and to their thinking. A good interviewer needs to listen to what the interviewee says. Otherwise, subtle information given in the interview is lost. Effective listening also helps develop an atmosphere of respect and acceptance of the other person's thinking.

To review, in order to help your students brainstorm interview questions and profit from this activity, follow these steps:

1. Model how you plan your interview questions.
2. Ask your students to plan their own interview questions.
3. Ask them what questions they might ask you as you play the role of interviewee.
4. Question your students about the questions they pose.
5. Make your students analyze the reasons for posing a given question.
6. Make your students aware that interview questions should have a purpose.
7. Make your students aware that good interview questions force the interviewee to think and speak about his or her thinking.
8. Model how you listen carefully during the interview.

▲ *The Peer Interview*

After role playing, brainstorming questions, and planning an interview, students are ready to begin to interview their peers.

Teachers who had their students practice peer interviewing found it helpful to do the following:

- Give students a word problem to work on.
- Ask students to solve the word problem independently themselves before planning their interview questions.

Once more, Susan's work will illustrate for us how these interviews might be organized.

What Susan Did

To train her students in their first opportunity to interview each other, Susan first provided her students with the following word problem:

There are 4 gerbils in the tank. Each of their paws is either white or black. Two have white front paws. One has 1 white front paw and 1 white back paw. One has no white paws. How many black front paws are there? How many black back paws are there?

After solving the problem individually, children were asked to pair up and interview one another. Let's read Sara's and Michael's interview.

> *Sara (S): How did you do this? Did you get any ideas from anybody else, or did you just do it by yourself and think of things by yourself?*
>
> *Michael (M): Well, I thought of things by myself, like I counted how many more . . . Here is what I did first. I was reading this and . . . I was reading it and there were, and I saw, I tried to get how many white paws there were. And then, I counted how many black paws.*

Notice that from Michael's explanation one can get an idea of how he solved the problem. First he counted the white paws and next he counted the black paws. We don't know about Michael's counting strategies. Did he count with his fingers or in his head? If we know that the gerbils were not actually present, then what did he count? Did he draw the gerbils, color their paws and then count them? There is much more to investigate. Let's see what Sara did next.

> *Sara: Oh, it is the same thing I did. And . . . did you take away the white paws in your head?*

One can see that Sara continued with a good question. She wanted to investigate how Michael did the counting. Yet, she may have given too much information in her question when she asked if he had done the operation in his head. Michael may have been induced to agree with the interviewer.

> *M: I kind of, like I was . . . I knew . . . First I started out with 2 front paws, because I knew there were 2, because that was there, and then I took 1 from the person that only had 1 white back paw and one white front paw, that was 3. And then, the others had 2 white front paws, so I kind of knew that was 3, because that was the only . . . [Sara interrupted him.]*

An interruption on the part of the interviewer can be dangerous because it is so tempting to put words in the mouth of the interviewee. Moreover, the interviewee's train of thought may be disrupted.

S: So, basically you counted all the black ones and left out the white ones?

M: Yeah.

Despite Sara's interruption, her question was a good one. She summarized what Michael was saying. It was a good summary, which also showed Michael that he was being listened to and that his ideas were clear for Sara. Let's see how she continued the interview.

S: What did you use?

M: I kind of did it in my head.

S: But, did you imagine the gerbils and stuff in your head?

M: Oh, yes, kind of . . .

From her questions, one can infer that Sara was not quite sure how Michael did the counting. The line of questioning she pursued to follow up on this issue was good. She used the word *imagine* to confirm if Michael had used a mental strategy. All in all, this was a fine first interview.

What You Can Do

The best way for your students to learn how to interview one another is for them actually to practice doing it. Keep in mind that your feedback is necessary in order to make sure that the task is being carried out productively. If possible, listen to the interview as it takes place. If you cannot be present in all of your students' peer interviews, be sure to find a way to record their interviews so that you can give them feedback later.

Whenever you ask your students to interview each other, be sure they understand the topic or content matter of the interview. The more knowledge the interviewer and the interviewee possess, the better the chances of a good interview. If not all of the students understand the topic, assign the role of the interviewer to the students who understand it better. Good questions are guided by the interviewer's knowledge; the well-informed interviewer knows what kind of information to look for.

As you teach your students how to monitor the effectiveness of the questions they have planned, model for them how you determine if a given question is accomplishing what you expected. Ask yourself aloud questions like these: "Did this question help me get the information I wanted?" "Why did this question work?" "Why didn't this question work?" Model for your students how you change questions when they don't work for you. Ask yourself out loud, for example, "How can I change this question to make it more effective?" Then go ahead and make the changes.

To sum up, have your students plan their interview questions, conduct their interviews, and monitor effectiveness as they go along.

To review, when your students practice peer interviewing, follow these steps:

1. Model how you plan an interview.
2. Model how you conduct an interview.
3. Model how you monitor the effectiveness of the interview questions as you conduct the interview.
4. Give your students a problem to solve.
5. Ask your students to solve the problem individually.
6. Ask your students to plan their own interview questions.
7. Pair up your students ensuring that one of them is knowledgeable about the content.
8. Ask your students to interview one another once they have finished solving the problem.
9. Find a mechanism to record your students' interviews if you are unable to listen to them directly.
10. Give feedback to your students regarding the peer interview.

▲ *Preparing Students to Discuss Peer Interviews*

The teachers with whom we worked videotaped or audiotaped their students while they were interviewing each other. As we have mentioned, this gave them the opportunity to give feedback to their students. Teachers also used the audiotaped and videotaped interviews to train their students further. Students learned new ideas about how to conduct an interview as they listened to their peers' interviews.

It is helpful to prepare students before they discuss taped interviews so that they are ready to learn from listening to their peers.

Teachers can prepare students to be productive listeners by doing the following:

- Ask students to brainstorm reasons for listening to peer interviews.
- Ask students to identify the questions they hear as they listen.

Let's see how Susan prepared her students for such a discussion.

What Susan Did

The following discussion took place in Susan's classroom:

> *T: Let me ask you why you think we are doing this today. Why do you think I am having you listen to this tape of the interview between Lisa and Charlie? Why am I doing this? There are a lot of reasons.*

Susan's question was a good one. Once again, she asked her students to think. She asked them to think about her reasons for engaging the class in the discussion.

> *Charlie (C): This was a very good interview.*
>
> *T: This was a very good interview. Yes, that's one reason. Absolutely right. Lissy?*
>
> *Lissy (L): If you get stuck when you are asking someone, you see the questions and the questions would tell you how to ask. Then you get it better.*
>
> *T: Lissy, can you repeat that? Stand up here, because I couldn't say it better myself, so everybody can hear you. Say it nice and loud.*
>
> *Lissy (L): Well, if when you see the questions from the tape you can get yourself more in a better position, by having the better questions to ask when you are stuck.*
>
> *T: Right. In other words, when you are interviewing somebody else and you get into a bad position. What other reasons? Two very good ones, it was a great interview and so the questions can help you when we are interviewing.*

Notice how Susan empowered her students by giving them credit for their ideas. In this way she established an atmosphere in which her students were comfortable in expressing their thoughts.

Each time that students are rewarded for sharing their thinking, they become even more likely to do it again.

Next, Susan urged her students to listen carefully for questions.

> **T:** *All right. I am going to rewind and then you are going to have to do your best listening. Now, you are now going to have to do your best listening. You are going to have to help me. Every time you hear Lisa ask a question, raise your hand and the minute I see your hand raised, I am going to stop the tape, so we can write that question down, all right? That's what we are going to have to do. How many questions do you think we are going to end up with?*
>
> **Peter (P):** *A million.*
>
> **Jane (J):** *Two million.*
>
> **T:** *Somewhere in between one and a million, I guess. Ready? Listen.*

Susan's instructions were clear, explicit, and detailed. Her students were ready to listen to a taped interview that concerned the following problem:

> There were 5 terrariums. Each terrarium had 5 seeds. There were bean and pea seeds:
>
> > #1 had 3 beans.
> >
> > #2 had 2 peas.
> >
> > #3 had 5 beans.
> >
> > #4 had 0 beans.
> >
> > #5 had 4 peas.
>
> How many beans were planted altogether?
> How many peas were planted altogether?

When Susan asked her students to tell her the questions they had heard, this is what she recorded:

> > How did you figure out your answer?
> > How did you get 3 + 3?
> > How did you get 12 + 13 altogether?
> > Using Unifix cubes?
> > How did you figure it out?
> > Can you get the Unifix cubes here?

What color did you use for the beans and peas?
What color is the beans and what color is the peas?
Blue is peas?
Why did you put it like that?
Why can't you go like that?
Let me see how you got your answer.

What You Can Do

Good teachers generally spend time at the beginning of an activity making sure that students know what they are going to do. The time spent giving instructions pays off. When instructions are not clear, time is wasted answering questions, students become anxious, and the classroom environment is disrupted.

Similarly, it is good practice to prepare your students to discuss peer interviews. Just listening to the interview, without having an understanding of the rationale underlying the questions, may not be enough to foster the development of interviewing techniques.

The preparation for a discussion can take many forms. Among them, teachers can ask their students to brainstorm their thoughts, they may guide their students' thinking with questions, or they may even tell students directly what the activity is and why they will be engaged in it. Your students will be much more motivated to carry out the activity if you make them think about the many reasons you could have to engage them in it.

Reinforce your students' positive contributions to the group. If you acknowledge their efforts and their growth, you will increase the likelihood of getting them to make good contributions more often. They all will benefit from reinforcement, acknowledgment, and encouragement.

To review, in order to prepare your students to discuss peer interviews, follow these steps:

1. Provide clear instructions.
2. Ask your students to think and brainstorm about the reasons you may have for engaging them in a discussion of peer interviews.
3. Get your students to listen purposefully as they identify the questions asked by interviewers.
4. Recognize your students' effort and the improvement in their ability to reason and think.

▲ *Thinking about Relationships among Peers' Questions*

As a next step in teaching students how to interview each other, teachers asked their students to discover patterns and relationships among the interview questions they had identified while listening to an interview.

As students find patterns among questions, they construct their own understanding about the characteristics of the questions and about how questions are asked. The patterns in the questions of an interview serve as guidelines for students' future questioning.

Teachers who carried out this task found it helpful to:

- Give students a list of interview questions in the sequence in which they were posed.
- Ask students to reflect on the relationships among questions.

Susan's work, once more, will be used to help explain how to carry out this activity.

What Susan Did

Let's take a look at a dialogue that illustrates how Susan guided her students to find patterns in Charlie's and Lisa's interviews.

T: Any patterns to these questions?

Sara (S): Oh, I realize something. Four of these questions have "How did you . . ."

T: So, now we know something about how questions are asked. Sara said that she noticed something, that the four questions we have so far start with "How did you . . . " That was a very good thing to notice.

John (J): Two have numbers in them.

T: All right. In two of them she is asking how he got the number sentences.

Notice that students easily began to find patterns. With practice they were able to find not only more patterns, but also more interesting patterns among questions.

Analyzing the sequence of questions is a step beyond identifying surface relationships among them. It involves an in-depth reflection about the order in which questions are asked and the reasons that they are asked. This kind of reflection allows children to become better interviewers. Students will learn that the questions in an interview are not arbitrary; there is a reason and a goal behind every question the interviewer asks. They will begin to recognize that the interviewer, hoping to learn about the interviewee's thinking, chooses certain questions in a certain order. In addition, they may also learn that in a flexible interview questions are often based on the interviewee's responses to previous questions.

As students construct their own meanings of the interview, they become better able to use the same kinds of questions later in their own interviews.

Susan continued to work with her students in finding relationships among questions. The dialogues that follow show how she did it.

> *T: So, in these two questions, what is Lisa talking about?*
>
> ***George (G):*** *How did he get the answer, or how did he get these number sentences?*
>
> *T: How did he get these number sentences? O.K. Why do you think Lisa went from, "How did you get 12 + 13 altogether" to asking, "Using Unifix cubes?"*
>
> ***Peter (P):*** *Oh, maybe he used Unifix cubes.*
>
> *T: How did she know that?*
>
> ***Sara (S):*** *She asked him.*
>
> *P: He probably told her that he had used Unifix cubes.*
>
> *T: Do you think that he already told her?*
>
> *S: I think he did.*
>
> *T: O.K. He did.*
>
> ***Charlie (C):*** *Maybe Lisa was just giving an example of something that he might have used.*
>
> *T: Why do you think she would do that?*
>
> *S: Well, then he could show her how he did it.*
>
> *T: Oh, because then he could show her with the material how he did it. O.K.*

We just saw how Susan read the questions and inquired about their sequence and goals. She also reflected, paraphrased, and challenged students' responses. In this way, she fostered a discussion among her students.

What You Can Do

You can ask your students to find patterns in questions. This exercise gives children the opportunity to think about *how* to ask questions. The patterns give them clues as to how questions are asked. It is important for them to see that an interview is more than a series of questions. They should be able to see that the questions are a tool used to assess and foster thinking.

You might begin by having students look at how the questions are alike in their surface structure, that is, in the language that is used. Ask questions such as, "Are these questions written in a similar way?" Ask students to note differences among questions, as well. Of course, patterns can be found at different levels. Once students are able to see relationships among questions, you can ask them to move from seeing surface relations to deeper ones.

If you want to get your students to analyze the sequence of questions and the rationale underlying it, ask them to reflect on a short list of questions. Have your students identify the purpose of each question. "Why did the interviewer ask this question?" "Why didn't the interviewer ask that question first?" Paraphrase your students' responses and challenge them.

Through your interventions, allow your students to draw their own conclusions about how the interviewer's purpose influences the way questions are worded and the order in which questions are asked. Allowing children to construct their own understandings is important in the thinking-oriented classroom. When students reason about the activities they engage in, they are more likely to understand them.

If you wish to ask your students to find patterns in interview questions, you may find it helpful to follow these steps:

1. Have your students listen or watch an interview.
2. Ask your students to identify the questions used in the interview.
3. Ask your students to discover relationships in the interview questions.
4. Ask students to find similarities among the questions.
5. Ask students to find differences among the questions.

6. Accept the contributions of your students, even if they refer to surface patterns.

7. Ask other questions that make your students think more deeply about the kinds of patterns among questions.

8. Ask your students to identify the purpose of each question.

9. Ask your students to discuss questions in the order in which the questions were asked.

10. Paraphrase your students' responses.

11. Challenge your students' responses.

▲ Learning to Write and Talk about Someone Else's Thinking

Keeping a written record of an interview has important advantages. It allows the interviewer to review what was said, in order to identify what is missing and which responses should be questioned further.

For the teacher, the written record is the tool that allows evaluation of students' thinking. It helps the teacher assess students' understandings, strengths, weaknesses, progress, and the gaps in their knowledge. Such a record also gives information about the ability of the interviewer to understand, explain, and summarize someone else's thoughts.

Teachers who taught their students how to record their peers' thinking found it helpful to do the following:

- Model how they would record someone else's thinking.
- Accept students' records as they were produced by children.

Many teachers have found that writing about a peer's thinking facilitates talking about that peer's thinking. Once a student has recorded an interview in writing, you may wish to ask the student to report to the class how the interviewee solved the problem. You will then have an excellent opportunity to assess the interviewer's ability to question his or her peer's thinking, understand it, and talk about it.

Students develop their own thinking as they talk about their peers' thoughts. As children hear the strategies their peers have used to solve a problem, they learn new approaches for solving it. As they compare their own strategies to those of their peers, they can use the comparison to improve their own.

Teachers who trained their students to talk about their peers' thinking found it helpful to:

- Ask their students to clarify and elaborate on their reports.
- Ask their students to talk about the other's strategies in terms of similarities with and differences from their own.

Once again, Susan's work will help explain how this activity can be carried out.

What Susan Did

In previous lessons, Susan's students already had learned to record their own strategies. Let's see how Susan explains to her students how to record the thinking of another student.

> *T: We have noticed that a difficult part of the interview is having to write down the answers. So, to get around that, we are going to experiment. We will have two people with the tape recorder, just talking to each other. The rest of you, I am going to give you paper. But, don't feel you have to write down every single word the person says. You can write down what they did, make a picture of what they did, something so that when you come back to the group, you will be able from your notes to tell the rest of the group what your person did. It doesn't have to be word by word. These are notes for you, so that when you come back you can say* [Makes believe she reads her notes], *"Well, Shawn used Unifix cubes, and he used orange cubes to show beans and white cubes to show peas."*
>
> *Students:* [Laugh]
>
> *T: O.K. I am just doing a pretend.*

This dialogue shows how Susan modeled the way she would have written someone else's strategy. Modeling is a useful teaching technique because it gives students the opportunity to see their teacher engaged in an activity similar to the one they are expected to engage in.

Let's take a look at children's written accounts of their peers' strategies. First, let's look at what Lizzy recorded about her own problem solving:

There are 4 gerbils in the tank. Two (2) have white front paws. One (1) has one white front paw and one white back paw. One (1) has no (0) white paws.

How many black front paws are there? 3

How many black back paws are there? 7

My strategy:

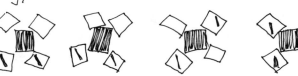

Let's take a look next at what Lisa wrote about Lizzy's strategy:

Name: Lisa

I interviewed Lizzy

He/she used this strategy:

First I took a brown cube for the botty. And every white paw I took a white cube. Every black paw I took a black paw.

Here is another example of a child's record of his own strategy. This is Justin's written account:

There are 4 gerbils in the tank. Two (2) have _white_ _front_ paws. One (1) has one _white_ _front_ paw and one _white_ _back_ paw. One (1) has no (o) white paws.

How many _black_ _front_ paws are there? _____

How many _black_ _back_ paws are there? _____

My strategy:

Date 4/10/91 _____   Name JuStin

Here is what Caleb wrote about Justin's strategy:

Name: Caleb _____
I interviewed ___Justin___
He/she used this strategy:
I drew pictures.
then I shaded the paws
that wern't white.
then I counted the
wons that wear
black

What conclusions can we draw about these students' thinking by judging writing samples alone? Students' written accounts of their peers' strategies certainly help clarify their drawings, but they are not complete. An oral report is very helpful in interpreting these written records.

Let's read next about how Susan taught her students to talk about another's thinking.

> **T:** *You talked a lot. Want to tell us about it?*
>
> **Robert (R):** *Sara used Unifix cubes. She said, "Well, if I had 3 beans, I know I would have 2 peas. Well, I used Unifix cubes and I made the red ones beans and the purple ones peas, because they help me figure out the problem and they are very, very fun to use."*
>
> **T:** *Oh, my goodness, so you really wrote down everything she said. Just like a tape recorder. That must have been difficult. Did you find that hard?*
>
> **R:** *No.*
>
> **T:** *Did you ask Sara any questions?*
>
> **R:** *Yeah. Why did she want to use Unifix cubes?*
>
> **T:** *And what was her answer to that?*
>
> **R:** *They are fun to work with.*
>
> **T:** *Did you understand her strategy, did she explain it to you clearly enough?*
>
> **R:** *Yes.*

As was discussed, one of the hardest things for children to do is to summarize the strategies used by the interviewee. We have seen how Robert copied verbatim what Sara had to say. Identifying and recording the most important information is not easy. Talking about someone else's strategy may be even harder. Robert read what he had recorded, but he did not summarize or comment on it.

Susan continued working with her students on how to express their peers' thinking.

> **T:** *Did anybody interview somebody who used a different strategy from your own?*
>
> **Michael (M):** *Shawn used a piece of paper, instead of anything else. He used a piece of paper and pencil.*
>
> **T:** *And what did you use, Michael?*
>
> **M:** *I used Unifix cubes.*

T: So you used two different strategies. All right.

M: Very different.

T: You want to tell me a little bit more about how Shawn did it?

M: Well, Shawn wrote the numbers down and he added them all up and then he got 12 + 13.

T: Can you say that again?

M: Well, you see, Shawn did it right. He wrote all the numbers down in a piece of paper.

T: Which numbers?

M: The numbers. You tell him, Shawn.

T: No, no, no. You tell him.

M: The numbers that were on the sheet. Like the first one had 3 beans or something, so he like wrote 3 + 2 and he added them all up and he got 13 + 12.

T: O.K. and did that make sense to you?

M: Yes.

T: O.K.

Notice how Susan encouraged Michael to think about and relate his own work to that of Shawn.

What You Can Do

Rather than giving your students a recipe to follow, model for them how you would record someone else's thinking. When students are not told explicitly how to carry out tasks, they have the freedom to construct their own ways of implementing them. They are more likely to derive meaning from them and internalize that meaning.

Learning to record someone else's thoughts is like learning to take notes. Because everything cannot be copied down, the most important information has to be identified. In the case of the flexible interview, the most important information is related to the strategies that the interviewee used. It is difficult to listen, to identify the most important information, and to record that information all at once. You may wish to teach your students how to record their thinking one step at a time.

First, once a few thoughts have been expressed by the interviewee, ask the interviewer to take a few minutes to write down what he or she has been told. Then direct the interviewer to ask the interviewee to continue the account. In this way, the interviewer does not take notes simultaneously, but only after listening to some ideas. Gradually, you can have your students attempt to take notes simultaneously, beginning by recording only a few minutes of talk and then adding on longer periods of time. To teach your students how to identify the most important information in what is being said, model how you, yourself, go about selecting what is important.

The first step in the process of learning to report after recording another's thinking is to read what has been copied. The ability to paraphrase develops with practice. To develop this skill in your students, be sure to give them multiple opportunities for practice, followed by feedback from you.

Talking about someone else's thinking is not easy. Not only does it require the identification of the most important information, but that information also has to be put in order and expressed verbally in a way that makes sense. Thus, just as you do when teaching children how to write about someone else's thinking, it is helpful to model for your students how to identify the most important information in order to talk about it.

Encourage your students to find relationships among the strategies they have used and those their peers have used. Ask your students to describe their peers' strategies in terms of similarities with and differences from their own. This is one way of getting students not only to talk about the interviews, but also to think about the interviews they have conducted.

To engage your students in learning how to write and talk about their peers' thinking, you may want to follow some of these steps:

1. Model for your students how you record someone else's thinking.

2. Model recording someone else's thinking.

3. Teach your students how to take notes after the interviewee has expressed a few thoughts.

4. Gradually, teach your students to take notes simultaneously as the interviewee expresses his or her thoughts.

5. Teach your students how to identify the processes and strategies that the interviewee used. They are the most important information in an interview.

6. Ask your students to compare their peers' strategies with their own.

▲ *Evaluating Task Performance*

Periodically, some of the teachers we worked with asked their students to express their feelings and thoughts about the tasks in terms of level of difficulty, motivation, interest, and the like. They were also asked to evaluate their performance on the tasks.

The evaluation of one's performance is a crucial component of skill development. Learners must be able to evaluate the tasks and their own work in order to improve it, modify it, and adapt it to their needs. This kind of self-assessment is what will make students aware of their needs and enable them to do something about meeting them.

Evaluation is important also because it can help the teacher obtain a good picture of students' strengths, weaknesses, and educational needs. These are valuable factors for the teacher to consider in planning future lessons and in tailoring them to meet students' needs. The kind of information obtained in an evaluation will enable the teacher to begin to relinquish the authority for the curriculum in the classroom and start to share this responsibility with students. There is no question that such an approach facilitates an open, collaborative environment in the classroom.

In addition, as children hear their peers discuss their difficulties, their own insecurities and feelings of inadequacy may be resolved. Students' self-esteem as learners may be enhanced as they note that others share similar needs.

Teachers who asked their students to evaluate their work found it helpful to:

- Conduct classroom discussions about the tasks they had carried out.
- Ask the students to identify the reasons why a task may have been easy or difficult.
- Accept individual students' perceptions of the tasks.

What Susan Did

Let's read next an illustration about how Susan went about guiding her students to analyze task difficulty.

> *T: You said that the interviews went good today. What was good about them? Did you find them easier?*

> **Carol (C):** I found them kind of easier, because it was so smooth. It was like, I am not sure. It was like if the new people or the way we were asking the questions made a difference. I am not sure.
>
> **T:** So, either it was that you were with a new person, or you are better at asking questions.
>
> **Sara (S):** I found it easier.
>
> **T:** How come?
>
> **S:** Because I wasn't the one that was interviewing.
>
> **T:** Who interviewed somebody and found it difficult to get the ideas going? Who found it a little bit more difficult?
>
> **Melody (M):** I kind of didn't understand Jacob. Like I said, "What did you do?" and he said, "I used yellow and green. I used green as my peas and yellow as my beans." And I don't really understand that because he didn't really explain the strategy to me.
>
> **T:** O.K. So, did you ask him questions to try to get more answers out of him?
>
> **M:** I did. I said, "Why didn't you use wooden cubes, blocks?"
>
> **T:** And what did he say?
>
> **M:** "Because I never used them before."
>
> **T:** The first time you did it, you found it frustrating for a lot of you. Some of you found it easier this time.

We can see that with her questions Susan encouraged her students to reflect carefully on their successes and failures.

What You Can Do

To allow this kind of evaluation to take place effectively in your classroom, pay special attention to keeping an open, risk-free environment. Such an environment will permit your students to speak openly about their thoughts and feelings in relationship to a task and in relationship to their own performance.

To encourage self-assessment in your classroom, question your students in a way that makes them reflect about their personal abilities and/or limitations, as well as about the strategies they have used and about the characteristics of the task they were engaged in. Ask questions such as these:

"What made the problem/task hard/easy for you?"

"Did you know all of the information needed to solve the problem?"

"What did/didn't you know in relationship to the problem/task?"

"How did you solve the problem?"

"What would have made the problem easier?"

"How could you have solved the problem/task more effectively?"

"What do you need to learn in order to carry out the task more easily?"

"What did you do that made the task/problem more difficult/easy to solve?"

"What would you do differently next time?"

Give your students an opportunity to talk about their positive as well as about their negative feelings toward the activity. To do this, ask questions like these: "How did you feel when carrying out the task?" "Did anyone feel frustrated while doing this activity?" "Who felt good while solving this problem?" "Why do you think you felt that way?"

Provide a chance for students to air frustrations, identify needs, and set new goals for the curriculum. Ask, for example, "What do you think our next activity should focus on?" "Which are the areas in which you think you need to work harder?" "How can we change the activity so that next time it is not that frustrating for you?" "In which areas do you need more practice?"

If you wish to get your students to analyze task difficulty, follow these steps:

1. Leave time for the discussion of tasks once they are completed.
2. Establish a risk-free environment.
3. Lead open-ended discussions in which children have the opportunity to talk about the tasks and about how they feel about them.
4. Ask questions that make your students reflect about their strengths and weaknesses, needs, and frustrations.
5. Give children an opportunity to have an input into the curriculum.

Thus far, we have discussed the most important activities that the teachers we worked with engaged in while training their students to interview each other. There is no question that there may be other techniques and/or activities that could be carried out with this same purpose. We encourage you to create your own way of training your students, modifying our work and making it meaningful for you. Only when you construct your own way of doing it will you feel comfortable carrying out the training sessions.

▲ *What Comes Next?*

Now that we have discussed how to interview students individually and in groups and how to teach them to interview each other, we will take a look at some general guidelines to help you prepare to conduct your own flexible interviews.

CHAPTER SIX

▲ *Guidelines for Flexible Interviewing*

As we have seen, flexible interviewing is a wonderfully powerful set of skills and ideas that can deepen your understanding of students and enrich your teaching. This chapter presents general guidelines for conducting flexible interviews, whether with individual children or groups of children.

▲ *State of Mind*

Flexible interviewing is not just a collection of techniques. At its heart is a set of basic assumptions, a belief system which motivates your whole approach.

Focus on Thinking

The first assumption is that the focus of the interview (and of the classroom!) is on thinking, not merely on right or wrong answers, not merely on parroting what the teacher says or what the textbook presents. How the child gets the answer to 23 × 4 is as important as, or even more important than, the correct answer itself.

The child's thinking makes sense.

Usually, the child's thought reflects a genuine attempt to make sense of the world and to create meaning. The meaning the child creates may not be the one that you intended to convey, but the child's thinking usually makes sense in its own terms. The child's belief that 12 − 4 is 12 is perfectly sensible—given key assumptions concerning the taking away of smaller numbers from larger ones.

As a teacher, you can make good use of your insights into the child's thinking. Although imperfect and requiring education, the child's thought can serve as a useful foundation for further development. The child's idiosyncratic method for getting the answer to 12 – 4 may not be the best way to get it, but you can use the child's method to lead him or her to a better way of doing and understanding subtraction.

Interpretation is key.

For the interview to be successful, you have to interpret the child's behavior. You have to develop hunches about what the child's behavior *means*. And to discover something meaningful, you must have some ideas about what to look for, some notions about the forms children's thinking may take. As Piaget put it, novice interviewers often "are not on the lookout for anything, in which case, to be sure, they will never find anything" (Piaget, 1976, p. 9).

What does this mean for you? Before interviewing, you must have at least a few ideas about children's mathematical thinking. Throughout this book, we have tried to present some basic notions that can help you interpret children's mathematics. These include ideas about *invented strategies*, *bugs* (or error strategies), and *understanding as connecting*.

Thus, Jennifer (described in Chapter 1) employed an invented strategy when she said, "Well, I know, well, I know that 3 and 3 is 6. And so, and so I know if I take 3 away from 6 you have 3 left." She had not remembered the answer, nor is it probable that she had been taught the method; she reasoned the answer by a process most likely of her own invention.

The child uses a bug when he claims that 12 + 9 is 111 because "2 and 9 is 11 and you put the 11 under the line and then you also put the other 1 there." Use of this bug makes the child's answer both predictable and understandable. It produces consistent behavior and leads him to get answers like 23 + 29 = 412 and 55 + 55 = 1010.

And understanding by connecting is illustrated by the example of Kathy, who was asked to compare 6 + 6 and 6 × 6. The interviewer asked, "Which one do you think will give you the biggest number for the answer?" She answered, "Well 6 × 6 is more than 6 + 6 'cause you have to count 6 times instead of only 2 times" (Ginsburg, 1989, p. 195). Kathy did not simply memorize the answers. She connected them with the method of repeated addition, which allowed her to understand multiplication and compare it to addition. Children assimilate what they are taught into what they already know.

These three concepts—invented strategies, bugs, and understanding by connecting—can take you a long way in interpreting children's mathematical behavior. In a way, these concepts require you keep in mind three fundamental questions:

- What method, whether taught or untaught, did the child use to get that correct answer?
- What was the line of thinking that led the child to produce that wrong answer?
- What does the answer mean to the child?

So interviewing is a very thoughtful activity, for both interviewer and child. In this respect (and many others, too) it stands in stark contrast to standardized testing. In the flexible interview, both adult and child need to think. The child needs to think about the problems, and the adult needs to think about what the child's behavior means. In the standard test, the child may have to think (not too much) about the problems, but the adult hardly needs to think at all. Standardized testing is easy for you to do, but of course that is not necessarily a good reason for doing it.

Can teachers successfully engage in the kind of interpretation required for flexible interviewing? Of course you can! You are always engaged in interpretation. You see how Barbara treats Mark on the playground and you interpret the behavior as indicating jealousy or hostility. You see Linda struggling with her multiplication tables and you interpret the behavior as indicating laziness or trouble with memorization or perhaps even a learning disability. You cannot get through a day at school without interpreting children's behavior. This does not mean, of course, that your interpretation employs some formal psychological theory. You do not say (and should not), "Linda cannot do this because she is in Piaget's concrete operational stage," or "Barbara is in Erikson's stage of autonomy." Indeed, such interpretations are virtually useless for teachers, and that is why teachers find little value in much of the formal psychology they learn in school (just as children often find little value in the formal math they learn in school).

Instead, you always interpret behavior by means of your own personal, practitioner's theory—your informal hunches about what makes students tick. To paraphrase Molière, you are thinking interpretation but don't know it.

All we ask you to do as an interviewer is to think more deeply about the meaning of children's mathematical behavior. How do they get their right answers and their wrong answers, and what does it all mean? How do they assimilate what they are taught into what they already know? And in thinking about these questions, we suggest that you begin by considering notions of invented strategies, bugs, and connected understanding.

▲ *Getting Started*

Though flexible, the interview is not completely spontaneous; you need to begin with a general plan and with some specific problems. Before interviewing an individual child, or a group of children, you need to make some preparations.

Develop a collection of problems with which to begin.

Before beginning, you need to work on a rough plan for the interview, including a list of tasks to present and questions to ask. The next chapter presents a collection of basic questions for key topics in elementary mathematics from grades K through 5. You can at least start with these and then develop your own.

You may obtain interview tasks from other sources, too: students' errors or questions, classroom problems and games, textbooks, other teachers, workshops, published materials, and your own imaginative inventions. One particularly useful approach is to draw on chapter examinations in textbooks or tests that you have devised. Test questions can serve as the basis for interview tasks to investigate student knowledge.

Whatever the origins of your tasks, you should not treat them as a standard test. Remember that you have the freedom to ask all of the questions on your list or only some of them. And, of course, you need not limit yourself to what is on the list. You may modify questions, drop some, and add others. That is, you should feel free to engage in nonstandardized flexible questioning. The problems should have several characteristics.

Focus on the child's current work.

If the class is now studying addition with regrouping, think of a few questions you might ask about the child's work on such problems. For example, "Why do you carry the 1 over there? What does that little 1 tell us? How much is it worth?" The questions should not require or lead to a yes or no answer, but should encourage open-ended responses.

Prepare specific tasks with which the child can engage.

Tasks should not be vague and unclear, leaving the child uncertain about what the question is and what needs to be done. Instead, tasks should present problems with which the child can grapple. Tasks should be focused and complex enough to challenge children and engage them in extended bouts of thinking.

The general rule is to make the task "specific." This can be accomplished in many different ways, in part depending on the topic and the developmental level of the child. In the case of younger children, you may wish to make concrete objects available. Don't just ask the child how we can figure out the answer to 7 + 2; present the child with blocks, chips, paper and pencil, or other materials that could be used to solve the problem. Manipulative devices can be very useful in flexible interviewing. Young children unable to work with an abstract task often can achieve success when the same task is represented with concrete objects.

But literal concreteness is not required; it is not always necessary to employ real objects. For older children, tasks involving written or spoken numbers are quite appropriate. You can ask how the child solves these tasks with paper or pencil or mentally.

What is most important is not necessarily to use concrete objects but to make the problem *specific* and *focused*, something into which the child can sink her (mental) teeth. In general, employ specific tasks that engage the child in familiar, everyday activities.

Vary the tasks.

Children can easily get bored with problems that seem to repeat themselves. In general, children do better with a variety of problems than with minor variations on the same theme. Therefore, try to vary the types of problems you give, the materials, the characters in stories, and the types of response the child is required to make.

Tasks that can be varied on the spot to suit the level of a broad range of students are very useful. One example of such a question is, "In how many different ways can you make 15¢ with coins?" When the value of the collection is changed to 85¢, the possible combinations are vastly increased, and therefore the question becomes appropriate for children at a higher level.

Prepare both open-ended and focused questions.

Although effective tasks tend to be specific, productive questions should at first be open-ended. They should give the child freedom to respond and allow the expression of personal ways of

thinking. One very specific suggestion is to avoid questions that require or permit a yes-or-no answer. Questions in open-ended form
are more likely to provide insights into the child's thought than
questions that can be answered by a simple "yes" or "no." "Tell me
how you added" allows for far more spontaneous expression than
"Did you add from left to right?"

Depending on what you discover in the child's response to the
open-ended questions, you can introduce a series of more focused,
directive questions to examine specific hunches about the child's
thought. In general, the sequence of questions should proceed from
general to more specific queries.

Get the equipment ready.

Once you have decided on the tasks, make sure that you have
readily available all of the equipment that the child might need in
the course of the interview: paper and pencil, blocks, toys—whatever is likely to be required. There is nothing worse (well, almost
nothing) than stopping an interview to hunt around for a toy or a
block for a certain task. By the time you have found the equipment,
you may have lost the child's interest.

Because they can display mathematical ideas concretely, manipulatives and records of student writing will facilitate your interviewing. They provide something that both you and a student can
see, move, and talk about. You can ask questions about what the
student is seeing, manipulating, and writing. Several manipulatives
are often available in schools: Unifix cubes, base ten blocks, or
Cuisenaire rods. Everyday objects also may be employed: coins and
food items such as popcorn, cookies, and fruit. Paper and pencil,
paper and marker pens, chalk and small chalkboards, grid or graph
paper, disposable hundreds charts, flipcharts, and designated student areas at the chalkboard all may be used for student writing.

Record the interview.

The interviewer needs to record the interaction in a form useful
for his or her purposes. Teachers generally do not find it useful to
record interviews on video or audio tape. For one thing, you do not
have the time to review them. In general, it is more practical to take
notes either during the interview or immediately afterwards. What
your notes contain depends on what you are interested in. They
may describe the child's major invented strategies, the child's bugs,
problems you wish to work on, ideas about lessons you might construct, or things to keep an eye on in the future.

Interview in a comfortable place.

The interview should take place in a reasonably comfortable place, quiet, well lit, and free of distractions. You might arrange interviews at a small table in the corner of the classroom. The rest of the class can work independently for those few minutes. Students look forward to a few minutes of their teacher's exclusive attention. The expectation that they, themselves, also will be interviewed motivates them to respect the requirement for relative quiet and self-management.

Some of the teachers we worked with even conducted interviews in the corridor outside the classroom. The location was not ideal, but it served the purpose. Everyone got used to it and learned to ignore the noise.

Sit close to the child, perhaps side by side, or perhaps at right angles. This may signal a less authoritarian relationship than does sitting opposite. Also, it makes it easier to read what the child writes (although many teachers easily read material upside-down). On the other hand, sitting side by side has at least one disadvantage: it makes it harder for you to see the child's face and thus to pick up signs of affect and the like. Sit where you feel most comfortable. The seating arrangement will not make or break the interview.

When to interview? One possibility is to work with students during a regularly scheduled "math choice" period. During that time the class may engage in enjoyable math games and activities that they already know how to do or that they can learn from classmates.

Which students to interview?

Your class may have students who differ from each other in many ways, including ability, style, experience, cultural heritage, attitudes, and beliefs about math. Some are confident, articulate speakers, some are good listeners, some are neither. Some love math while others fear it. You will discover that interviewing almost always reveals exciting and useful information no matter which student is interviewed.

Bright, articulate students often are excited to talk about their thinking, and you will be excited to learn about what they are doing. Their good reasoning and communication skills can help an entire class learn to talk about thinking.

Students who seem to lack both ability and confidence will sometimes amaze you with a creative and original way to think about a problem. You will find unsuspected skills and abilities hidden in your weaker students. Those skills and abilities offer a foundation on which you can build further.

The rather silent middle of the class—students who understand well enough, behave well enough, and do well enough in written work—often receive less of a teacher's attention than they deserve. They may surprise you too.

▲ *Motivating the Child*

To do well in an interview, the child needs to be comfortable and motivated. There are several things that you can do to encourage this.

Empathize and support.

Children are often placed in the subordinate position of being judged by an adult. They worry about getting wrong answers or appearing stupid. You must try to counter these feelings and to allay the child's anxiety. You can do several things to help. First, you must attempt to empathize with the child's feelings. Try to understand how the child must feel about the interview. Don't assume that the child automatically sees it as an enjoyable or even non-threatening experience.

Second, you can try to be warm and supportive. Show that you recognize that the child may be nervous about the interview and act in a comforting manner. Remember—you are dealing with a child who is likely to feel threatened.

In supporting the child you have a secret weapon. The very fact that you as an adult attend respectfully to what the child says, the fact that you show an interest in the child's thinking and ways of looking at the world—all of this relaxes the child and enhances motivation.

Explain the purpose of the interview.

The general goal is not simply to put the child in a good humor or to encourage relaxation or compliance with the interviewer's demands. Rather, the goal should be to create a special relationship between interviewer and child, a relationship of trust in which interaction revolves around the child's thinking.

You need to establish, if your classroom hasn't already, that the interview does not involve evaluation, grading, and the like. Even though you and the child may be very familiar with one another, the child may not have had experience in speaking with you and other adults in a flexible and open-ended kind of dialogue. You need to reassure the child that you are interested in how he or she solves problems, not on whether the answer is right or wrong.

Explain that the interview involves a focus on thinking. For example, "I will talk with you to find out how you do your math. I want to know how you think about it. If I can find that out, I might be able to help you do better at your math." No doubt, the child will not understand everything you say and may wonder why an adult would want to know about his or her thinking. Indeed, the child is likely to come to an understanding of the interview only after having some concrete experience of it. At the same time, you will have accomplished a great deal if only you get across the general attitude that you respect the child enough to try to explain what you are about. But whatever you say, make it simple and honest.

Use the child's language.

Often, when children talk about arithmetic in their own language, they do not use the proper adult words. They say "take away" instead of *subtract* or "times" instead of *multiply*. But don't mistake their poor language for misunderstanding of the concepts. (Conversely, don't mistake correct language for conclusive evidence of real comprehension.)

Indeed, you might even want to use the child's language yourself, even if it is "wrong," in order to foster communication. Say "number" instead of *numeral* if it will help you to understand what the child knows. You can (and should) teach the conventional usage later on.

Put the child in the role of expert.

The child is more likely to reveal thinking if he or she is placed in the role of expert. And, of course, the child *is* the expert on his or her own thinking. How to do this? One way is to say that you are trying to learn about how children think about their math and that you need help. Another is to ask the child to offer a make-believe explanation of some topic to a younger child: "Suppose that you want to explain to your younger brother why we add this way. How would you do that?" or "Suppose you wanted to teach a younger kid the best way to do his homework. What would you say?"

Of course, putting the child in the role of expert means that you have to accept the role of novice. Some teachers are not used to this, but it is good for them and for the child to realize that teachers don't know everything and the child can be an important resource.

Don't discourage the child's way of solving problems.

Do not discourage the child's methods of solving problems, even if they are unorthodox. If the child wants to solve a problem mentally or by using fingers or by some other unconventional method, you must accept the child's approach. Remember, the first goal is to learn what the child is thinking. Later you may wish to teach the child another method, but first you need to find out how the child spontaneously approaches the task. So encourage the *child's* method; yours can come later.

Focus on what the child can do.

You should enter the interview with the assumption that the child is capable of doing some interesting work. Even if the child has been experiencing difficulty with some topics in school, don't assume that he or she knows nothing. Try to locate the child's strengths; focus on what the child *does* know.

To establish a mood of confidence, start with a task that is reassuringly easy. Let the child begin by doing well, by demonstrating competence. Do not begin by placing the child in a failure situation. If the child seems to have trouble with the initial task, change it right away; make it simpler so that the child can succeed without too much trouble.

Avoid runaway tasks that dominate the interview. Whenever a task is obviously too hard or is beginning to take over the interview, you might say, "We have spent enough time on this task. Let's choose another." Try not to let a hopeless task drag on and on.

It is also important to let the child conclude the interview with a feeling of success. After you have done the major work of the interview, during which the child will probably have to struggle a bit, return at the end, as at the beginning, to some relatively easy problems.

Encourage effort.

You want to make sure the child is attending to the tasks you present, is working hard, and is trying to deal with them in a serious way. The major way to encourage such motivation is to praise the child for effort, for engagement, for thoughtfulness. General statements like "You're doing a good job" or "I like the way you think about your math" or "You had some interesting ideas about that one" are appropriate. Certainly you should put more emphasis on praising effort and thoughtfulness than on rewarding correct answers (or punishing incorrect ones).

How much encouragement is needed? Unfortunately, as in the case of many other aspects of the flexible interview, the answer is: it depends. Some children require a good deal of encouragement and praise; others do not. Some may even require some pushing or other forms of pressure. Individual differences in motivation are enormous among children at the same age. But teachers deal with issues like these all the time. You have to judge on the spot what kind of encouragement or discipline is appropriate for the individual child.

Focus on process, not product.

In general, you do *not* want to say, "Good. That was the right answer." Such an approach may divert the child's attention from thinking; indeed, it may reinforce the tendency to worry about the right answer. Similarly, it is generally not a good idea to say, "No. That's the wrong answer." This may devalue the child's method of solution, which in fact may be quite sensible.

On the other hand, there are important exceptions. Sometimes, particularly in the case of children who are capable of success but careless, it may be useful to acknowledge the child's failure in a very explicit fashion: "That was wrong. I know you can do it. Try again. Think about it this time." Similarly, when the child is well aware of and discouraged by failure, you may say: "I saw you were having a hard time with that one, but that's O.K., I'm more interested in how you solve the problems than in whether you get them right or wrong." Or: "You got that one wrong. But that's a hard problem that most first graders don't get. Anyway, what's more important is how you think about it. . . . "

Perhaps a useful general rule is this: don't talk about right or wrong answers if doing so will cause the child to focus only on the answers themselves (rather than the process) or serve to discourage the child. But feel free to talk about right and wrong answers if doing so helps to promote thinking.

Monitor affect.

Throughout the interview, you must constantly monitor the child's emotion. You need to be aware of the child's anxiety, delight, interest, boredom, and the like.

Encouraging the child to understand and express feelings about learning should be a key aspect of education. It is very difficult for all of us to say, "I feel lost and confused," or "I don't understand," or "I feel bad because I don't know this." On some deep level, we must feel that our missteps in the course of learning signal deep personal inadequacies. Beginning in childhood, we need to learn to understand, express, and place in perspective feelings like these. As a teacher, you can give children some help in doing this.

Encourage verbalization.

Don't assume that you know what the child is thinking. You certainly don't want to put words into the child's mouth; indeed, you want to take words out of the child's mouth. You have to encourage the child to verbalize as fully as possible in response to your questions. As we saw in Chapter 2, there are several ways in which you can help children to learn to examine their own thinking and to talk about it. This should be one of the major goals of education for young children.

Dealing with "Difficult" Children

From the interviewer's point of view, children may be "difficult" in several ways. Some children are extremely shy and reluctant to interact with the interviewer. But gentle patience, persistence, and approval usually suffice to put the shy child at ease and encourage some degree of communication.

A second type of "difficult" child is one whose cultural background does not permit or encourage children to speak freely with adults, or at least with "different" adults from another group. What to do in this case? First, don't assume that the silence is the result of ignorance. Instead it may indicate an attempt to engage in respectful behavior as defined by the cultural group. Second, patience and empathy often can help you to get through to the child. After all, communication between very diverse groups is still possible with a minimum of good will.

Very rarely you will encounter a child who is boastful and vain, an obnoxious showoff. With such a difficult and sometimes uncooperative child, the best policy is basically patience and clear focus on the child's specific activities, not on his or her putative talent or giftedness.

The Priority of the Personal

Individual differences among children abound, and you as interviewer therefore have to treat each child in a unique way. Some children profit from a good deal of structuring; others require an open-ended approach. Some children need gentle encouragement; some children need to be told to work harder. The attempt to respond to differences like these is both the strength of the flexible interview and its major weakness. It is hard to treat each child appropriately, each according to his or her needs. Doing it requires real sensitivity to personal nuances.

▲ *Examining What the Child Knows*

We come now to the heart of the flexible interview—examining the child's thinking. The interviewer is always trying to find out: Why did the child make that response? What did the child mean by that statement?

Ask the fundamental question.

One way to learn the answers to these questions is to ask how the child solved the problem. The fundamental question of flexible interviewing is: "How did you do that?" Of course, this generic query needs to be varied in many ways that may be useful for different children, different ages, and different situations. Here are several possibilities:

"Can you do it out loud?"

"How did you figure that out?"

"Can you show me how you did it?"

"How do you know?"

"How would you show it?"

Some children are timid and refuse to volunteer their approach, perhaps because they think you may not approve of it. In this case, you might ask the child to discuss examples of other children's work: "Here is how another kid in your class solved the problem. Here is what he said about how he did it . . . What do you think about that?"

All of these questions are designed to encourage children to talk about their ways of solving problems. Of course, some children find it harder to do this than others. It is easier for older children than it is for younger ones to talk about their thinking. You have to be patient; it may take some time and consistent work in class before children are prepared to tell you much about their thinking.

Think about the meaning of the child's behavior.

Listen to what the child says. Think about what it means. Consider the reasons for the child's answer. Did the child get the wrong answer because he or she did not understand your instructions? Did he or she get the answer by counting or by simply remembering the number facts?

Don't assume that a wrong answer necessarily implies lack of knowledge. Sometimes, when the child gives an incorrect answer, it may be the result of an interesting line of reasoning, a result of assumptions different from those that motivated your question. Indeed, the child's "wrong" answer may really be the "right" answer to a different question, a question you did not ask.

Similarly, don't assume that a right answer always implies understanding. It may indicate mere memorization or parroting. The general rule is to look for the meaning underlying the child's answer. Always ask yourself what sense it might make. You will find that analyzing the child's behavior is one of the most interesting and rewarding parts of interviewing.

So if you listen carefully and think about what you hear, you can become a good interviewer.

Shh!

On some occasions, a very important interview technique is to say nothing, to ask no questions. Give the child enough time to think and work out his or her methods of solution. The flexible interview should not be a pressured, rushed situation. There is no need to hurry. The child needs to learn that you are not interested solely in quick, correct answers, but instead take seriously, and indeed encourage, attempts to think things through. By waiting, you are counteracting a misconception that many children entertain about mathematics, namely that it requires quick responding without thought. Children need to learn to think carefully, to deliberate. So wait, and then maybe just ask the question again before going on to something else.

Echo and reflect.

On some occasions, the technique of *reflection* may elicit interesting material. Instead of asking directly, "How did you do it?" or the like, you simply repeat or echo the child's last statement. If the child says, "You add them this way," you simply wait a while and repeat, "You add them this way," perhaps with a slight questioning tone. Under these circumstances, children often elaborate on the thought and tell you more about their method of solution.

Ask the child to prove that the answer is right.

Sometimes the child has difficulty in talking about a method of solution, or may not even realize that there is a method of solution. For example, the child says that 5 + 4 = 8 and does not know how he or she got the answer or even that there could be a sensible way of getting the answer aside from memorizing it. When this happens, you can ask the child to prove that his answer is correct: "How do you know that 5 and 4 is 8? How could you prove it to me?" Or: "How could you make sure you are really right about that?"

This type of question encourages the child to think about the issue, perhaps for the first time. It may help the child to talk about the method of solution if he or she has one. If not, it will help the child to realize that there are almost always sensible ways to solve mathematical problems and that relying on memory is not the only solution.

Explore.

Often the child responds in unexpected ways; the answers do not fit the interviewer's existing categories. What to do? The strength of the flexible interview is that it allows the interviewer to explore the child's way of thinking. After all, the ultimate issue is not what the interviewer has in mind; it is what is on the child's mind. So if the child does or says the unexpected, explore it. Follow the child's response wherever it leads. If the child gives an unconventional reason for doing something, ask for an explanation. Responsiveness to the child not only can lead you to the underlying thought, but also may contribute to the child's positive motivation.

Observe.

Despite your best efforts, some children may not say (and cannot learn to say) very much about their thinking. But there is more to the flexible interview than recording and evaluating answers to questions and other verbal material. Watch what the child does. You can get some hints about the child's thinking by observing how she is using her fingers, or what she says when she whispers to herself, or what numbers in a written problem she looks at or crosses out first. Look also at the child's pauses, pace, gesture, facial expression. Overt behavior often reveals a good deal about thought.

Probe.

After you have some idea about how the child solves the problem, you may wish to confirm your hunch. Suppose you know that Matthew is adding by counting on, but are not sure whether he counts from the first number or from the larger number. To check this possibility, you may then give some special, contrasting problems, like $8 + 3 = ?$ versus $2 + 9 = ?$. Doing this little "experiment" should give you the information you need. In general, you need to introduce critical problems and variations in order to decide among alternative interpretations of the child's behavior.

The Three Deadly Sins

Consider next three "don't's"—interview sins that should usually (with reference to the flexible interview, never say "never") be avoided.

Don't talk too much.
The child should do most of the talking, not you. Of course, you have to be active, asking penetrating questions. But you should spend most of your time listening to what the child has to say and observing. If you are talking more than the child, something is wrong.

Don't ask leading questions.
Phrase your question in a neutral way so as to avoid suggesting an answer to the child. Don't say, "Why is this answer wrong?" Say instead, "What do you think of this answer?" Don't say, "Why didn't you carry here?" Say instead, "What did you do to get this answer?"

Don't correct and teach.
Your ultimate goal, of course, is to help the child learn mathematics. But you must often suspend that goal during the flexible interview. You must refrain from correcting and teaching. Don't say, "No, you're wrong; this is how to do it." Don't show your disapproval by grimacing or scowling. Instead, you should give the impression that you are interested in what the child said, even if it is wrong, and that you want to find out more about it. As a teacher, you may find it difficult at first to suppress the impulse to correct a child's mistakes. But if you wish to have deeper understanding of the child's thinking processes, you must allow the child's erroneous beliefs and unproductive strategies to be expressed freely and without constraint. You should not forget that your major goal is to determine how the child achieved the incorrect answer, not to correct thinking (which in fact might have been very sensible). Later on, you will have an opportunity to use what you learned in the interview to help the child.

Of course there are exceptions to every rule—at least, to every rule of interviewing. Suppose that you discover that a child lacks some concept or is employing a seriously flawed strategy. Suppose further that the child realizes that there is something amiss and looks to you for help. Under these circumstances, can you refuse to help? Doing so may constitute a violation of the trust you have established with the child. You know the child needs help and the child knows it too. How can you refuse to teach? One simple solution is to tell the child that you still have some questions to ask but will help later on.

▲ *What Is the Child Really Capable Of?*

There are two different situations in which you want to probe the limits of the child's competence. In one case, you have been interviewing a child who has not been performing very well, but you hesitate to conclude that she really does not know the material. You wonder: is this the best she can do? Have you been able to get an accurate view of the limits of her knowledge?

The second situation is very different. The child gives a correct answer, but you have the feeling that her success is more apparent than real. She may not really understand her answer or the means for obtaining it. Does the correct answer really indicate an underlying understanding?

In both cases, you want to find out whether the child's performance accurately reflects underlying competence. Is the failing child capable of a higher level of performance? Several methods are useful for investigating this issue: asking the child to repeat the question, rephrasing the initial question, changing the task, repeating and reviewing problems, returning to simpler problems, and probing. Is the second child's success genuine? You may find out by employing countersuggestion.

Consider first the child who has done badly but may possess an underlying competence.

Ask the child to repeat the question.

Suppose the child does not seem to know how to deal with one of your questions. Perhaps the child says, "I don't know," or uses an immature strategy. One possibility is simply that the child has misunderstood the wording of the question.

You may find out by asking the child to repeat the question or, better still, to reformulate it: "What was the question I asked you? Tell me in a different way." Or: "Tell me what I'm asking you to do." The child's response may point to a misunderstanding that can easily be corrected.

Rephrase the question.

Another approach is to rephrase the question. Say it in another way. Use different language, even using the child's incorrect mathematical terms like "Can you times it for me?" (Later on, after you have discovered whether the child understands the concept, you can correct the child's language.) Of course, it is sometimes difficult to rephrase questions on the spot. But this may help. When you are preparing basic problems before the interview, try to think of three or four ways of rewording each basic question.

So, if the child gets a wrong answer to one of your questions, entertain the possibility that you haven't yet found the right wording and that when you do the child's competence will be revealed.

Change the task.

Another tactic is to change more than the wording. Change major features of the problem itself. Make it different, or more specific, or more concrete. Some children will do better with concrete manipulatives than with written problems. Some will do better with abstract mental problems than with manipulatives. You never know what will work; be flexible enough to try almost anything.

Repeat and review.

Another approach to a child's failure is basically not to accept the wrong answer. Instead, ask the child to do it again. You can repeat the problem and ask the child to explain carefully and slowly how she solved it, what she thought about it, and so forth. You can say, "I didn't quite understand what you meant, so let's do the problem over again and this time, try to tell me again how you are doing it. Let's go over it more slowly this time." Sometimes this sort of careful review helps the child to work through superficial difficulties and display competence.

Return to simpler problems.

If the child fails at a problem and does not seem to know what is going on, one technique is to go back to simpler problems on which she can succeed, and then gradually introduce more complex problems, eventually arriving at the problem that the child initially failed. Sometimes this process will help the child to understand what the more difficult problem requires and will even lead to success.

Probe.

Another approach to resolving ambiguity about competence is to ask further questions, to probe, to dig deeper, all in an effort to clarify the child's response and to gain deeper insight into her thought. You need to say things like, "What did you mean by that?" and "Tell me more."

Offer countersuggestions.

Finally, consider the case of the child who *seems* to have done well but may not really possess the competence suggested. True, she got the right answer, but several aspects of her behavior may make you wonder whether she really understands. If you suspect that the child's answer is superficial, challenge it. One approach is to present a "countersuggestion"—that is, a verbal contradiction of what the child has just said. Suppose that the child maintains that order of multiplying makes no difference (commutativity). But you suspect that the child is merely parroting what you have said and does not understand the principle at all. You might say, "No, that doesn't work for 9's." Now, of course, this suggestion is absurd, and the child who really understands commutativity will stick with her answer and even explain it. But the child whose understanding is superficial may well accept the wrong answer merely because you suggested it.

▲ *Determining What the Child Can Learn*

The bottom-line question for teachers is whether and under what conditions the child can learn particular material. Suppose that you have examined the child's way of thinking about division. You know what the child does and does not understand; you have some insight into how the child approaches division problems. Now your questions shift to learning potential. Is the child capable of learning various aspects of division?

You might investigate this issue on two different levels. First you might ask about the child's ability to profit from the minimal help provided by hints. Can the child pick up the concepts or master the strategies with only minor assistance? At the other extreme you might ask: how does the child respond to more directed, but brief, teaching? Does he or she assimilate it well, thus indicating that more sustained instruction can be profitable?

Provide hints.

Hints do not "give away" the answer. They convey information that is only indirectly relevant to solving or thinking about the problem. Thus, if the child is having difficulty adding, you might say, "Think about putting these groups together" or "Is there anything you already know about adding that can help you here?" or "How could counting help you to do this?"

If the child responds quickly and successfully to hints, at least two interpretations are possible. One is that the child already knew the material and the hints simply helped him or her to understand what was required and to use what was already known. A second possibility is that the child was already close to knowing the material, and the hints merely provided a slight impetus to complete the process. In either event, the child's successful response to hints demonstrates a clear ability to learn the material in question.

Teach.

Teaching is more elaborate and structured than hinting. Teaching, in the sense of direct instruction, provides information that is directly relevant to solving the problem. Such teaching involves explaining to the child directly and explicitly that multiplication can be thought of as so many groups of *n* objects each or that the algorithm for multiplication involves such and such procedures. You already know that the child you are interviewing has difficulty learning multiplication in class and that simple hints do not help him or her to learn the material. The question now is whether focused, individualized teaching in the context of the flexible interview will help the child learn the relevant concepts and procedures. If such teaching is effective, then at least some degree of learning potential has been demonstrated and you may be able to find ways to continue instruction in the context of the classroom.

▲ Epilogue

So much for the guidelines. Now, three final points.

First, remember that this is not a cookbook, but only a collection of general suggestions. It is important to note that interviewers vary in their styles of interviewing. Some interviewers tend to praise or ask direct questions or probe more than others. Interviewers differ in their abilities too. Some interviewers are better than others at encouraging the shy child or monitoring the child's affect. So don't feel that there is just one way to interview. You need to find your own "voice," and the only way to do that is to take the leap—talk to the students, do the interviews.

Second, even the most experienced interviewer never conducts a completely successful interview. In a sense, you never finish the interview. You always wish that you had said something different. You always think of something that you could have said. You almost never learn as much as you would like about the child. But even if your interview is imperfect, as it must be, you are likely to learn something about the child's mind, and the child might, too.

Third, if you implement interviewing in your teaching and assessment of students, your role as a teacher will probably change. You will still plan your lessons carefully, but they will often take unexpected directions. You may no longer feel a need to protect your students from knowledge of their mistakes. You will help your students develop a tolerance for ambiguity and a willingness to take risks.

With this in mind we leave you with "The Ten Commandments of Flexible Interviewing." Chapter 7 presents specific questions you can use as a basis for interviewing.

The Ten Commandments of Flexible Interviewing

1. Prepare an initial protocol containing specific tasks with which the child can engage.

2. Convince the child that your focus is on the process of thinking, not merely the answer.

3. Encourage and support the child's effort, spontaneous verbalization, and personal ways of solving problems.

4. Make sure that the child understands the instructions and general requirements of the task.

5. Probe the child's thought, asking *The Fundamental Question*: "How did you get that answer?"

6. Begin with open-ended questions and gradually make them more specific, always adjusting your questions to the needs of the individual child.

7. Observe what the child is doing as he or she solves the problem.

8. Explore, following the child's thought where it leads.

9. Ask the child to *prove* that the answer is correct.

10. Always think about the meaning of the child's behavior.

CHAPTER SEVEN

▲ *A Sampler of Questions*

Guidelines are not enough. You need specific questions to ask your students. This chapter presents sample questions to use for assessment and teaching.

Perhaps your students are working with topics and concepts different from those involved in the preceding chapters. Or you may be looking for questions related to a particular student's current needs. In this chapter you will find examples of questions related to many of the concepts or big ideas learned in elementary school mathematics classrooms from kindergarten through fifth grade. You may use the examples in this chapter as a basis for developing your own questions, making them easier or more challenging depending on your needs.

If you were to make a list of the big ideas in elementary school mathematics, the list would not be very long. The order of the counting numbers (2 is greater than 1 and 3 is greater than 2) is a big idea. Place value (a 6 in the tens column is worth 10 times as much as a 6 in the ones column) is a big idea. The commutative property of addition ($5 + 3 = 3 + 5$) is a big idea. The idea of a reciprocal ($\frac{3}{4} \times \frac{4}{3} = 1$) is another big idea. There are a few others.

The following chart specifies the major concepts or skills and the grade levels at which they often are learned. The same big ideas appear again and again in different combinations. A good interviewer knows which important concepts or big ideas are relevant to a task. By asking questions that focus on big ideas, you will gain insight into how to help your students. Follow-up teaching can be tailored to their particular needs.

As you have seen in the previous chapter, questioning to assess thinking goes beyond just finding out whether students are able to get the right answer to a problem. If you ask questions that explore the student's reasoning and use of strategies in relation to the underlying big ideas, you will learn what students think while they are doing math and how well they understand important concepts.

Big Ideas in Mathematics: Grades K–5

	Grade Level					
Big Idea	*K*	*1*	*2*	*3*	*4*	*5*
Counting numbers	X	X	X	X	X	X
Place value	X	X	X	X	X	X
Addition and subtraction	X	X	X	X	X	X
Geometry	X	X	X	X	X	X
Multiplication			X	X	X	X
Division			X	X	X	X
Fractions			X	X	X	X
Primes and composites				X	X	X
Decimals					X	X
Ratio and percent						X

Kate, a second-grade teacher, told us, "Good key questions and some structure make the interview more efficient. Without key questions, it is possible to listen to a child talk for half an hour without learning anything useful."

Now let's look at some questions that attempt to investigate students' understanding of some of the big ideas in elementary school math. First, let's look at questions relating to the counting numbers themselves.

▲ *The Counting Numbers*

Counting

You know that counting makes a one-to-one correspondence between the counted objects and numbers used to count them. This object is called *one*, that object *two*. There is only one way to arrange the counting numbers from least to greatest. We say "1, 2, 3" not "1, 3, 2." And each number is one more than the number before it. By adding 1 to any number we can get a larger number, and we can keep going on and on toward an infinitely large number. Often it is useful to skip-count by 2's, 5's, or 10's.

Those are some of the big ideas related to the sequence of the counting numbers. You can use tasks and questions like those that follow to investigate your students' understanding of the counting numbers.

Counting Task #1
Ask the student questions about the counting sequence.

Q. How high can you count?

Q. Do you know what comes next? How did you figure it out?

Q. How do you know that 10 comes after 9 (or any other numbers)? Why can't 9 come after 10?

Q. What number is between 6 and 8? How did you figure it out?

Q. Which is more, 11 or 12? How do you know that?

Q. What comes next: 11, 12, . . . (or any other numbers)?

Counting Task #2
Present students with two sets of blocks or tiles. Beside the first set write the numbers 13, 15, and 12. Beside the second set write the numbers 15, 18, and 16 (see the example that follows). Ask the student to draw a circle around the number that represents the quantity within each set.

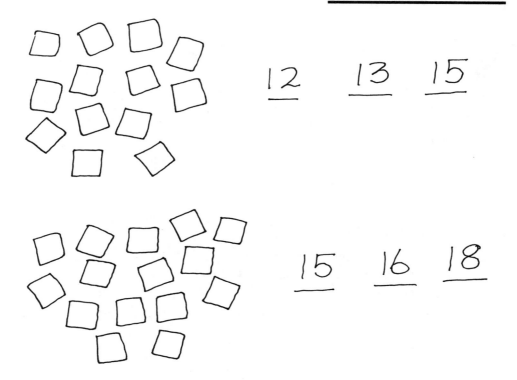

Ask students:

Q. How do you know you circled the correct number beside each set?

Q. What can you do to make sure you counted each object only once?

Q. Is there another way you can check that you counted each object only once?

Q. How could you prove that your answer is correct?

Counting Task #3

Show students lists of even numbers. Write them horizontally, and include at least six numbers in each row:

4   6   8   10   12   14   16

14   16   18   20   22   24

Ask students:

Q. Do you see a pattern in these numbers?

Q. Do the numbers come in a certain order?

Q. What do you notice about the last digit of each number?

Q. Are the numbers that usually come before and after 22 on this list? Why are those numbers not on the list?

Other Counting Tasks

Q. Is 6 closer to 7 or to 4? Explain how you figured it out.

Q. Is 18 closer to 10 or to 20? Explain how you know that.

Q. Tell me all the even numbers between 15 and 27. How did you know where to start? How did you know which numbers to skip? How did you know where to stop?

Q. Which is more, 273 or 269? How do you know? What are some ways to tell which of two numbers is larger than the other?

Q. Can you count from 24,998 to 25,006?

Q. What is the largest number that you can name? How long do you think it would take to count up to that number?

Practice with estimation helps students to get a better intuitive understanding of the value of large numbers.

Q. Estimate the number that is halfway between 16 and 52. Figure out the answer exactly. How did you arrive at your estimate? Were you close? If you were not close, how could you be close next time?

Q. Estimate the number of classrooms in the school (the number of books in the bookcase). How could you make your estimate closer?

Q. Estimate the number of pennies in the jar (the length of the ball field). How could you find the answer without counting all the pennies? (measuring the whole field?) How could you check your estimate?

▲ *Place Value*

The big ideas relating to place value are simple. Probably because we have ten fingers to count on, our number system is a decimal system. We can represent any counting number by using the ten digits 0 through 9. Each place or position in the number has a value that is 10 times as great as the value of the position to the right of it. You can use questions like those that follow to investigate your students' understanding of place value.

Place Value Task #1
Ask students to write the following numbers from dictation: 9; 99; 999. Then ask:

Q. What do you notice about the numbers you just wrote?

Q. How many digits are there in the first number? the second number? the third number?

Q. What number would come after 9? after 99? after 999? Do you see a pattern?

Q. What value does each of the 9's have in these numbers? If they have different values, what makes them different?

Children sometimes write the number 109 as 1009, or 100 followed by 9. If this happens, ask:

Q. Write the number 109. What value does the 1 have in the number 109? Does the 1 in your number stand for 100, less than 100, or more than 100?

Q. Can you prove that you need four digits to write the number 109?

Place Value Task #2

Q. In the number 275, which digit shows the number of ones? Tens? Hundreds? Show how you would represent the number 275 with base ten blocks.

Q. If you wanted to add 5 to that number, show how you would do it with the blocks.

Q. If you wanted to show the number 380 with the blocks, what would you need?

Q. If you had 4 more flats (hundreds) what number would you have made with the blocks?

Q. If you took away 2 longs (rods, tens), what number would you have left?

Place Value Task #3

The following task can be tailored to your students' level. Often the question is easy to answer for small numbers but more difficult with larger numbers. Therefore, you may wish to warm up with small numbers and ask progressively more difficult questions with larger numbers.

Q. What number comes after (before) 20? 25? 29? How did you figure it out? How could you explain to a little child how you figured it out?

Q. What number comes after (before) 200? 250? 299? How did you figure it out? How could you explain to a little child how you figured it out?

Q. What number comes after (before) 2,000? 2,050? 2,099? How could you show that you are right?

Other Place Value Tasks

Q. What does the 6 stand for in the number 64? 156? 632? 16,700?

Q. How many 10's make a 100? 300? Explain your answer using base ten blocks.

Q. How many 10's are needed to make a 1,000? How did you figure it out?

Q. What is the largest two-digit number? Three-digit number? Four-digit number? What is the smallest two-digit number? Three-digit number? Four-digit number?

It is especially difficult for many students to read and write numbers with zero in one or more positions. Sometimes we write numbers in expanded notation to help students understand their value. The number 304 can be written in several ways, including:

- three hundreds and four ones
- 300 + 4
- (3 × 100) + (0 × 10) + (4 × 1).

Q. Write in expanded notation: 64   278   1,285   70   503   4,060. Explain how you did it. What does the 0 stand for in the number 70? In the number 503? How can you show that you are correct?

Q. Read (write) these numbers: 250   2,145   2,070   50,604.

Often we round numbers to make them easier to compare. Sometimes we round numbers to make it easier to estimate their sum, difference, product, or quotient.

Let's look at some questions involving rounding numbers:

Q. Round the number 624 to the nearest ten. Explain how you did it.

Q. Round each of the numbers 74, 75, and 76 to the nearest ten. Explain how you did it. Did you get the same answer all three times? Explain why or why not.

Q. How could you use rounding to estimate the sum of 63 and 79? To what number did you round the 63? The 79? Why?

Q. Use rounding to help you estimate the sum of 6,782 and 8,357. Did you round to the nearest ten, the nearest hundred, or the nearest thousand? Which choice will give you an estimate closest to the actual sum? Why do you think that is true?

▲ Addition and Subtraction

Addition and subtraction often are thought of as combining and separating. To state it very simply, addition combines or joins parts to make a whole, while subtraction separates that whole into its parts. Activities that combine or separate groups of blocks or coins or buttons, for example, or stories that present real-world situations, help students model addition and subtraction.

Addition/Subtraction Task #1

Present the students with a die (with sides numbered 1–6) and some small blocks. Ask students to roll the die, read the number, and take that number of blocks. Again ask them to roll the die, read the number, and take the appropriate number of blocks. Next, ask students to tell you how many blocks they have altogether. You might ask:

Q. How did you figure out how many blocks you have altogether?

Q. Can you find another way to tell how many blocks you have altogether? Prove that you have that many blocks.

Addition/Subtraction Task #2

Place a tray with candies in front of a group of students. Ask one student to eat one. Next, ask the students to count how many candies are left. Repeat this exercise with each student in the group. Ask:

Q. What did we do? Explain how you know what we did.

Q. If we took away one more candy, how many would be left? [*Take it away.*]

Q. What would happen if we put the candy back into the tray? [*Put it back.*] How did the number of candies change when one candy was put back?

As children begin to learn about addition and subtraction, they gradually develop familiarity with the basic addition and subtraction facts. Looking for the many patterns and relationships among the number facts helps students to learn the facts without heavy reliance on rote memory. What are the big ideas that children use to find sums?

The order rule (commutative property) means that the order of the addends does not matter when we are finding a sum. If students know $3 + 5 = 8$, then they can know also that $5 + 3 = 8$.

If students know that $10 + 3 = 13$, then they can use the grouping rule (associative property) to find that $8 + 5 = 13$ as well. They just take 2 from the 10 and group (associate) it with the 3 to make 5.

The zero rule (identity element for addition) tells us that we can add zero to any number without changing its value; $5 + 0 = 5$.

Finally, addition and subtraction facts come in fact families. Because subtraction is the inverse of addition, if $3 + 4 = 7$ and $4 + 3 = 7$, then 7 – 3 = 4 and 7 – 4 = 3. Knowing any one of the four facts in this fact family enables students to know the other three.

Many children discover those big ideas by themselves. Other children need help from the teacher.

Here are some questions to ask about the basic addition and subtraction facts and how they are related.

Addition/Subtraction Task #3

Present students with a picture of a triangle with the digits 7, 3, and 4 (or another combination) written in each of its corners, respectively, and the addition and subtraction symbols written at the center:

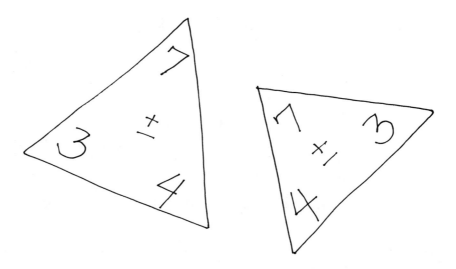

Ask students to look at the triangle. Ask them:

Q. How are the numbers in the triangle related?

Q. When you add 3 + 4, is the answer the same as for 4 + 3?

Q. Make up an addition story problem using the three numbers 3, 4, and 7. Draw a picture to illustrate your story. Can you make up a different addition story using the same three numbers? Can you make up a subtraction story using those same three numbers? Which is easier to make up, an addition story or a subtraction story? Why?

Addition/Subtraction Task #4

During the course of class discussions or in conversation with an individual student, ask students to explain to you how they can find an unknown fact from a known fact. For example, if a student knows that 3 + 3 = 6, ask how the student can figure out the sum of 3 + 4. If a student knows that 9 + 2 = 11, how can that be used to find the sum of 2 + 9? Regularly ask students to explain to you how they can show that a sum or difference is correct. Whether a student says that 5 + 3 = 8 or that 5 + 3 = 9, ask the student to show how he or she figured it out. Just talking through an explanation often will help students either to strengthen their confidence in the strategy they used or to discover an error.

▲ Addition, Subtraction, and Place Value

Some of the big ideas for addition and subtraction already have been discussed in relation to number facts. Besides those, the most important big idea relates addition and subtraction to place value. Because we have a place value system of writing numbers, students must understand *exchanging*, or *regrouping*, or *trading*, or *carrying* and *borrowing*, to use a few of the most common names for the process of moving from one column to the next in multi-digit addition and subtraction. As this procedure is better learned, students are able to compute problems with larger and larger numbers.

Subtraction from a number with zeros in it presents a particular difficulty for many students. Work with base ten blocks can be very useful in helping those students.

Let's look at some questions to investigate addition and subtraction using place value.

Addition/Subtraction Task #5

When children write a problem from the board or from dictation, they often fail to put the digits of a number in the proper column. Then they add the wrong digits. For example, when adding 23 + 5, the student may begin by putting the 5 under the 2 and get the answer 73. If this happens, you may wish to ask:

Q. How could you prove that your answer is correct?

Q. Add 23 + 5 without using pencil and paper. Did you get the same answer? Is one answer better than the other? Why?

Q. What is the value of the 3 in the number 23? Of the 2? Of the 5 in the number 5?

Q. When you add, does it matter where you place your numbers? Where do you usually put the ones digit? Where do you put the tens digit?

Q. Would you like to write the problem again in a different way? How will you write it? Find the answer the new way. Which answer is better, the new way or the old way? Why do you think so?

Other Addition/Subtraction Tasks

Next we present a variety of problems involving estimation, rounding, and mental addition. After that we describe further fundamental interview questions to help you explore students' responses to these problems.

Q. Explain how you might use rounding to help you estimate the answers to these problems:

34 + 52   36 + 53   28 + 79
60 – 19   56 – 21   42 – 17

Q. Use mental arithmetic to figure the change from $1.00 for an item that costs 39¢.

Q. Find the change from $5.00 for an item that costs $2.85. Show how to use base ten blocks to check your answer.

Q. Suppose that your friend said that $3.00 minus 65¢ is $2.45. Can you find your friend's error? Why do you think that error was made? How could you help your friend understand how to find the correct amount?

Q. There were 14,635 families living in a town. 5,742 families owned dogs. How many families did not own a dog? First estimate your answer. Explain how you estimated. Then find the exact answer. How good was your estimate? Explain how you could check your answer.

Q. Here are the areas of the four Scandinavian countries:

Denmark has 16,580 square miles.

Finland has 130,127 square miles.

Norway has 124,556 square miles.

Sweden has 173,426 square miles.

Which is the largest Scandinavian country? Which is the smallest? Estimate the total area of the four Scandinavian countries combined. Explain how you arrived at your estimate. Use a calculator to find the exact answer. Was your estimate a good one? Could you have made your estimate closer? How?

Here are some fundamental questions you can use to explore further students' responses to the tasks above and, of course, to any other tasks.

Tell me how you did that.

Why is that true?

How did you reach that conclusion?

Does that always work? Why or why not?

How could you prove that?

What assumptions are you making?

What would happen if . . . ? What if not . . . ?

Do you see a pattern? What is it? Explain.

How did you think about the problem?

How is your method like hers? How is it different?

How does this relate to . . . ?

What ideas that we have learned before were useful in solving this problem?

When students are working together, you can ask questions like:

What do you think about what Richard has said?

Do you agree? Disagree? Why or why not?

Does anyone have the same answer but a different way to explain it?

▲ *Multiplication*

We have noted that young children use counting to help them add. Because multiplication can be thought of as repeated addition, many children begin to learn multiplication by skip-counting. Counting by 3's gives the multiples of 3, for example. Other patterns in the multiplication table also are related to patterns in the addition table.

Like addition, multiplication is governed by the order rule (commutative property) and grouping rule (associative property). $3 \times 4 = 12$, so $4 \times 3 = 12$. And if we know that 4×6 equals 24, then we can divide 4 by 2, take that two and group (associate) it with the 6 to make 12. In other words, $4 \times 6 = (2 \times 2) \times 6 = 2 \times (2 \times 6)$, which leads to $2 \times 12 = 24$ as a result.

There are a few other big ideas about multiplication and division. Multiplication has its inverse operation, division. Therefore, you can divide to reverse a multiplication. The identity element for multiplication and division is not 0, but 1. Thus, $2 + 0 = 2$, but $2 \times 1 = 2$. Multiplication and division by 1 do not change the value of the number. Multiplication by 0 always results in 0. We do not divide by 0.

Multiplication and division have fact families, just as addition and subtraction do. If $2 \times 3 = 6$, then $3 \times 2 = 6$ and $\frac{6}{3} = 2$ and $\frac{6}{2} = 3$.

Multiplication has one other property that helps students learn their facts and also prepares them for two- and three-digit multiplication. That idea is the distributive property. The distributive property means that you get the same answer if you multiply 9×3 all at once, or if you break 9 up into two or more parts, multiply 3 by each of those parts of 9×3 and then add up the partial products that result. Because $9 = 4 + 5$, then (9×3) equals (4×3) plus (5×3). This is useful. If you know the facts 4×3 and 5×3, you can use them to find 9×3, like this: $12 + 15 = 27$.

Here are some questions about relationships among multiplication and division number facts.

Multiplication Task #1

Ask students to give you the answer to a simple fact problem, such as 6×8. Whether the answer is right or wrong, follow up with related questions.

Q. How could you use addition to find your answer?

Q. How could you use skip-counting (by 6 or by 8) to find the answer?

Q. Does your answer help us to find any other related fact? How does your answer help us to find 8×6?

Q. Show with tiles or blocks a rectangle that shows the product of 6 × 8. How can you use the rectangle to show the product of 8 × 6? Explain why this is so.

Q. Are there other ways to make a picture of multiplication?

Q. What three other facts are in the family with 6 × 8?

Q. Explain how you find the other facts in a fact family.

Q. Which facts (in the 6 table) are the most difficult for you to remember? Why are they so difficult? What could you do to make them easier for you?

Multiplication Task #2
Special multiplication facts are related to the square numbers.

Q. Build these products with tiles or blocks: 3 x 3   4 x 4   5 x 5. What are the products? Why are these numbers called square numbers?

Q. Color in all the square numbers on a hundreds chart. What pattern do you find? How many square numbers are on your chart? What is the smallest square number? What is the largest two-digit square number on your chart?

Q. Tell me what you know about square numbers.

Multiplication Task #3
Ask students to solve these two problems and then ask the suggested questions:

- 2 children each have a bag of chocolate bars. There are 4 bars in each bag. How many bars are there altogether?
- 4 children each have a bag of chocolate bars. There are 2 bars in each bag. How many bars are there altogether?

Q. In what ways are the two problems alike? How are they different?

Q. Do both problems have the same answer? Why do they (or do they not) have the same answer?

Q. Explain how you got your answer to the first problem. Then explain how you got your answer to the second problem. Did you solve them both in the same way? Why or why not?

▲ *Multiplication and Place Value*

In addition to those big ideas that we already have discussed in relation to multiplication facts, there is bad news and there is good news. The bad news is that multiplication with large numbers requires some method for working with place value. The good news is that the distributive property helps us to do this.

We already have seen how the distributive property helps find simple multiplication facts like 3×9. It is even more useful for multiplying larger numbers. Multi-digit numbers can be written as a sum of smaller, one-digit numbers. Each of those smaller numbers can be multiplied, one by one, and the products can all be added together to give the final product. For example, the problem (7×16) can be written $(7 \times 10) + (7 \times 6)$. By extending this method, students can find the product of any two whole numbers, however large. The distributive property is the basis of our standard algorithm for multiplication, as well as the basis for what is called the partial-product method, often taught in schools. It is also the basis for most of the multiplication strategies that students invent. If students learn to multiply numbers by multiples of ten ($6 \times 3 = 18$, $60 \times 3 = 180$, $600 \times 3,000 = 1,800,000$), they will better understand the multiplication algorithm and be better able to estimate answers to problems.

You can ask questions like the ones that follow to assess your students' ability to use place value and multiplication together.

Multiplication Task #4
Ask students to solve the following problem:

The distance from Tony's school to his house is 800 meters. How many meters will he walk in a week if he walks back and forth every day, Monday through Friday?

Q. How did you figure that out?

Q. How else could you have figured it out?

(If the student first used multiplication, ask him or her to solve the problem using addition or subtraction. If the student first used addition, ask if the student could solve the problem using multiplication or division.)

Q. Why did you not use division (subtraction) to solve the problem?

Multiplication Task #5

Q. Here are two problems that look alike. Multiply 40 × 60. Then, multiply 40 × 50.

Q. Explain how you got your answer to the first problem.

Q. Now explain how you got your answer to the second problem.

Q. [*If both answers are correct*] Your answer to the second problem has one more 0 than your answer to the first problem. Are you sure that you are right? Show me that your answers both are right. Why is there one more 0 in the second answer?

Q. [*If either of the answers is not correct*] Are you sure that you are right? How could you check your answers to see if they both are right?

Multiplication Task #6

Ask your students to solve this problem:

Three friends went to a restaurant. Each spent $7.95. How much did they spend altogether?

Q. Estimate the total cost of their meal.

Q. Show how you could use play money to find the answer.

Q. Using pencil and paper, find out exactly how much they spent.

Q. How could you prove to a friend that your answer is correct?

Q. Show another way to find the answer. Which way do you prefer? Why is it better?

Other Multiplication Tasks

Q. Write and solve a word problem for 12 × 35 = ? for 50 × 68 = ?

Q. Multiply 400 × 2,000 in your head. What were you thinking while you were finding the answer? Check your answer with pencil and paper. Did you get the same answer? If not, which answer is right? Find your mistake. Explain how to fix it.

Q. A recipe for cake calls for an 8 × 8 inch square cake pan. You have two rectangular cake pans: a 7 × 9 inch pan and a 6 × 10 inch pan. Which of your two rectangular cake pans will be a better size to use with your recipe? Explain how you decided which pan to use.

▲ *Division*

Just as subtraction is the inverse of addition, division is the inverse of multiplication. In multiplication we have two factors, and we are looking for their product. In division, we have the product and one factor, and we are looking for the missing factor. Often division does not come out evenly; a remainder is left.

The commutative and associative properties that are true for multiplication are not true for division. It is not true that $6 \div 2 = 2 \div 6$. It is not true that $(24 \div 6) \div 2 = 24 \div (6 \div 2)$.

Let's look at questions relating to division, with special attention to remainders.

Division Task #1

Q. 3 pigs ate 15 apples. Each pig ate the same number of apples. Draw a picture to go with this story.

Q. How could you explain your picture to a friend?

Q. How many apples did each pig eat? Were any apples left over?

Q. How did you figure out the answer?

Division Task #2

Q. Show with blocks: $19 \div 4$.

Q. How did you decide how many groups of blocks to make? Are all of the groups the same size?

Q. Is there a remainder? What does the remainder tell you?

Q. 4 people are dividing 19 candy bars among them. How much candy will each person get? What will they do with the remainder? What else could they do with the remainder?

Division Task #3

This task attempts to see how well students understand the concept of a remainder.

Q. Divide 124 by 7. Find the answer to the problem. What is the remainder?

Q. Next divide 125 by 7. What is the remainder this time? Can you use your answer to predict the answer to the problem $126 \div 7$?

Q. Divide 126 by 7. Was your prediction correct? Why or why not?

Q. Predict the answer to the problem 127 ÷ 7. When you divide a number by 7, can the remainder ever be larger than 7? Why or why not?

Q. What is the next number greater than 126 that is evenly divisible by 7? How did you find it out?

Division Task #4

The concept of equivalent division problems is often useful in estimating quotients. This task explores that concept. An equivalent division problem can be created by multiplying (or dividing) both the divisor and the dividend by the same number. For example, (8 ÷ 2) = (80 ÷ 20) and (700 ÷ 200) = (7 ÷ 2).

Q. Divide 35 by 5. Divide 350 by 50. Divide 3,500 by 500.

Q. Did you get the same answer? If not, recheck your work.

Q. Were you surprised that those three problems all have the same answer? Explain why the three different problems have the same answer.

Q. Make up a related division problem that has the same answer. Check to see if you are right. Then explain how you predicted that the answer would be the same.

Other Division Tasks

Q. Make up a story problem for 1,660 divided by 76. Estimate the answer. Find the answer. Check the answer. What did you do with the remainder when you were checking the answer? Is this a difficult or an easy problem? Explain why you think it is easy or difficult.

Q. Estimate: 35 ÷ 12   204 ÷ 5   6,301 ÷ 20. Check your estimates with a calculator. Were you close?

Q. In a class there were 25 children. 14 of them were 9 years old. 6 were 10 years old. 5 were 8 years old. Make a graph to show the ages of the students. Estimate the average age of the students in that class. Find the average age to see if your estimate was correct.

▲ *Prime and Composite Numbers*

Ideas about prime and composite numbers are very closely related to ideas about multiplication and division. Familiarity with prime and composite numbers helps students develop number sense and makes them better estimators. The ability to factor numbers is a skill necessary for working with fractions and, later on, for factoring algebraic expressions.

What is a prime number? It is a number that can be divided by only two numbers, itself and 1. We say that it has *exactly* two factors, the number itself and the number 1. The number 2 is prime; it has exactly two factors, 2 and 1. The number 1 is not prime; it has only one factor, 1. The number 4 is not prime; it has three factors, 2, another 2, and 1. The first five positive prime numbers are 2, 3, 5, 7, and 11. There is an infinite number of prime numbers.

What is a composite number? Any whole number that has more than 2 factors is composite; it can be composed in different ways. For example, 6 has the factors 1, 2, 3, and 6. It can be thought of as 6×1 or as 3×2. The first five positive composite numbers are 4, 6, 8, 9, and 10.

Both prime and composite numbers can be either positive or negative. If 5 is prime, then –5 is prime. If 6 is composite, then –6 is also composite.

The number 1 is special; it is neither prime nor composite. It is the building block from which all the counting numbers are made.

It is important to know that there is only one prime factorization of a whole number. For example, the prime factors of 20 are {2, 2, 5}. There is no other set of positive prime numbers that can be multiplied to make the number 20.

Here are a few interesting tasks relating to prime and composite numbers.

Primes and Composites Task #1
Ask your students to write the following list of numbers on a sheet of paper: 2   4   7   8   10   11   15   16   17   18.   Then ask:

Q. Which of the numbers are prime?

Q. How could you tell which of those numbers are prime numbers?

Q. Is there another way to find out which numbers are prime?

Q. How could you prove to a friend that 11 (or some number the student has said to be prime) is a prime number?

Primes and Composites Task # 2

Students learn to use different methods to find the prime factors of a number. One common method is to use a factor tree. Another method is to divide repeatedly by prime numbers, starting with 2, until no more even divisions can be made. Those two methods are shown in the following diagram:

18

③ 6   or   ② 9

②③   ③③

         9
    ②)18   2)18
       ③   3)9
    ③)9   3

All methods give the set of prime factors of 18 :
$$\{2,3,3\} \text{ or } \{2,3^2\}$$

Q. Find all of the prime factors of the number 18.

Q. Explain how you did it.

Q. How can you prove that there are no more prime factors?

Primes and Composites Task #3

Q. List all the factors (both prime and composite) of 10, of 24, of 25.

Q. Which has the most factors?

Q. Which has the fewest factors?

Q. Show with blocks or tiles how you can find all the factors of those numbers.

Q. Can you explain why 24 has more factors than 10 and 25 do?

Q. Predict which will have more factors: 18 or 21. Give reasons for your prediction. Check to see if your prediction was correct.

▲ *Fractions*

Many big ideas are involved in the understanding of fractions. Some of them will have been introduced gradually beginning in kindergarten, when students work with halves and fourths as they divide sandwiches and fruit. Learning about fractions involves learning new meanings for fractions, the concept of equivalent fractions, the idea of a reciprocal, and computation with fractions. We will look at these four topics one at a time.

The Meanings of Fractions

Fractions refer to parts of a whole or parts of a group; half of an apple or half of a box of 8 crayons. Fractions also are number names; the fraction $\frac{1}{2}$ names a point on the number line halfway between 0 and 1. Fractions may indicate division; $\frac{3}{4}$ indicates the number of cookies per person when 3 cookies are divided among 4 people. Fractions also refer to a ratio; if 3 out of every 5 students in a class are girls, then girls make up $\frac{3}{5}$ of the class. Fractions with any of those meanings can be added or subtracted, multiplied or divided in the same way, but they must be understood in different ways.

It is no wonder that students find fractions mystifying. It is particularly mystifying that when you multiply two whole numbers, the answer is greater than either of them, but when you multiply a whole number by a fraction less than 1 the answer is *smaller* than the original number, and when you divide a whole number by a fraction less than 1, the answer is *larger* than the original number. Students are required to modify their ideas about multiplication and division in order to incorporate this new concept. Here are some questions about meanings of fractions.

Fraction Task #1

Ask students to use paper folding to demonstrate their answers to the following questions. First let them experiment with the paper. If they need help, show them how to fold the paper.

> Q. How many fourths does it take to make a half? Show me with your folded paper.
>
> Q. Can you write that with pencil and paper?
>
> Q. Is there another way to show that ²⁄₄ make ½?
>
> Q. How many fourths does it take to make a whole?
>
> Q. Show with your paper how much ¾ is. Which is more, ²⁄₄ or ¾?
>
> Q. Which is more, ²⁄₄ or ½? Can you prove your answer?

Fraction Task #2

Ask students to solve the following problem: Susan had 3 apples. She ate half of one of her apples. How many apples were left?

> Q. How did you figure out your answer?
>
> Q. Draw this story on paper. How does your drawing help you explain your answer?
>
> Q. How do you know that your answer is correct?

Fraction Task #3

Ask students to find the answer to the problem: Peter ate ¼ of a cake that weighed 1 pound. Jonathan ate ¼ of a cake that weighed 2 pounds. Each boy ate ¼ of a cake. Did they eat the same amount of cake?

> Q. Draw and label the 2 cakes. Show how much each boy ate in your drawing.
>
> Q. What answer did you get? How did you figure it out?
>
> Q. How do you know that your answer is correct?

Other Fraction Tasks: The Meaning of Fractions

Follow up the tasks that follow with some of the fundamental questions suggested earlier.

> Q. Draw a diagram showing a pizza divided into 8 equal slices. Shade in 3 slices. What fraction names the shaded portion of

the pizza? What fraction names the unshaded portion? What fraction names the whole pizza?

Q. At a birthday party there are 12 children. 7 of them are girls and the rest are boys. Write a fraction that shows what part of the children are girls. Then write a fraction that shows what part of the children are boys.

Q. Draw a number line. Mark 0, 1, and 2 on the number line. Draw points on the line to show $\frac{1}{2}$, $\frac{1}{4}$, $\frac{3}{4}$, and $\frac{5}{4}$.

Q. Arrange these fractions in order from least to greatest: $\frac{1}{3}$, $\frac{2}{3}$, $\frac{1}{2}$. Explain how you did it.

Q. Which of these fractions are greater than 1?

$\frac{1}{2}$ $\frac{3}{2}$ $\frac{3}{4}$ $\frac{7}{4}$ $\frac{5}{5}$ $\frac{9}{5}$ $\frac{2}{3}$

How can you tell which they are? Is any of those fractions equal to 1?

Q. Write a percent that is equal to: $\frac{1}{4}$, $\frac{1}{2}$, $\frac{3}{4}$, $\frac{4}{4}$.

Q. There are twenty candies in a bowl. Half of them are chocolate. One-fourth of the candies are peppermint. The rest are lemon. How many candies are chocolate, how many are peppermint, and how many are lemon? Make a pie chart to show the assortment of candies in the bowl.

Equivalent Fractions

The idea of equivalent fractions is surprising to students who until now may have known only one way to write a number. Equivalent fractions make addition and subtraction of fractions easy. They also enable us to reduce fractions to lowest terms and to compare two fractions to see which is larger.

You can ask the following questions to investigate your students' understanding of the very important concept of equivalent fractions.

Fraction Task #4

Q. Write three fractions that are equivalent to $\frac{3}{4}$.

Q. How did you do it?

Q. How do you know that they are equivalent?

Q. Are your three equivalent fractions also equivalent to one another? How could you show that?

Q. In your own words, what does *equivalent* mean?

Fraction Task #5

Using equivalent fractions is a good way to solve a proportion:

Q. Make equivalent fractions to find the value of *x*:

$$\frac{1}{2} = \frac{x}{6} \qquad \frac{3}{5} = \frac{6}{x} \qquad \frac{1}{7} = \frac{x}{21}$$

Q. How did you figure out which numbers to use for *x*?

Q. Could you make up another problem like these?

Q. How would you explain to a young child how to solve your problem?

Other Fraction Tasks: Equivalent Fractions

Q. Find a common denominator and use that denominator to write equivalent fractions for the fractions $\frac{2}{3}$ and $\frac{3}{5}$. How did you figure out what number to use for a common denominator?

Q. What is the least common denominator for $\frac{2}{3}$, $\frac{3}{5}$, and $\frac{3}{4}$? Using the least common denominator that you have found, compare the three fractions. Arrange them in order from least to greatest.

Q. Reduce to lowest terms:

$$\frac{5}{15} \qquad \frac{6}{9} \qquad \frac{24}{40}$$

How did you do it? How did you figure out what number to divide by?

Reciprocals

Every number that can be expressed as a fraction has a reciprocal. The reciprocal of 17 (which can be thought of as $\frac{17}{1}$) is $\frac{1}{17}$, the reciprocal of $\frac{1}{2}$ is $\frac{2}{1}$ or 2, and the reciprocal of $\frac{3}{4}$ is $\frac{4}{3}$.

The product of a number and its reciprocal is exactly the number one. Because division is the inverse of multiplication, division by a fraction is the same as multiplication by the reciprocal of that fraction. $8 \div \frac{2}{3}$ is the same as $8 \times \frac{3}{2}$. Reciprocals are useful in simplifying algebraic expressions.

Let's look at two questions about the concept of a number and its reciprocal.

Fraction Task #6

Q. Write the reciprocal for:

$$\frac{1}{4} \qquad \frac{5}{3} \qquad \frac{2}{3} \qquad \frac{7}{1}$$

Tell in your own words how to find the reciprocal of a number.

Q. Multiply $\frac{1}{4}$ times its reciprocal. What is the answer? Multiply $\frac{5}{3}$ times its reciprocal. What is the answer? Predict the answer you will get if you multiply $\frac{2}{3}$ times its reciprocal. Do the multiplication. Was your prediction correct?

Q. What is a reciprocal?

Q. Tell what you know about reciprocals.

Operations with Fractions

Now that you know what your students understand about the meaning of fractions, you can investigate their thinking as they perform operations with these useful numbers.

Fraction Task #7

It is useful to provide students with manipulatives as well as pencil and paper when they learn to perform operations with fractions.

Q. Use fraction pieces to show how you can add $\frac{1}{2} + \frac{3}{4}$. What is your answer? Explain how you figured it out.

Q. Do the same problem using pencil and paper. Explain what you wrote.

Fraction Task #8

This problem investigates students' understanding of the concept of multiplication or division when one of the factors is less than 1.

Q. The school day is 6 hours long. One class period is $\frac{3}{4}$ of an hour. How many periods are there in the school day?

Q. Use fraction pieces or draw a picture to illustrate this problem. Show how you got your answer.

Q. [*Ask this question if the correct answer, 8, is given.*] There are only 6 hours in the school day. But your answer is greater than 6. Can you explain why you think it is possible to have more periods than there are hours in the school day?

Q. [*Ask this question if the answer given is not 8.*] All right. You said that there are _____ periods in the day. And each period is $\frac{3}{4}$ of an hour. Show how that adds up to a 6-hour day.

Other Fraction Tasks: Operations with Fractions

Q. A rug is 2½ yards long and ¾ of a yard wide. Draw a picture of the rug and label the lengths of its sides. Explain how you find the area of a rectangle. What is the area of the rug? How did you find it? Did your answer surprise you? Why or why not?

Q. Subtract 1⅕ – ⅘ using fraction pieces. Then do the same problem using pencil and paper. Explain your work.

Q. A spool holds 7 yards of ribbon. ⅓ of a yard is needed to tie a bow. How many bows can be made with the whole 7 yards? How could you check your answer? Take this piece of string. Measure and cut a piece 7 yards long. Cut it into pieces each ⅓ of a yard long. Show that your answer is correct.

▲ *Ratio and Percent*

Ratio

A ratio shows the relationship between the size of two quantities. Often ratios are written as fractions. The ratio 40:100 or $^{40}/_{100}$ shows the relationship between 40 and 100. 40 is $^{40}/_{100}$ of 100. Ratios are often used to make scale models and maps. A ratio of 1:10,000 means that every inch or centimeter on the map represents 10,000 of those same units in the real world.

Here are two questions about the rather difficult concept of ratio.

Ratio Task #1

Q. A cake recipe calls for 3 cups of sugar for each cup of butter. Draw a picture showing what is needed for this recipe.

Q. Write a ratio to compare the amount of sugar needed to the amount of butter needed.

Q. Pretend that you have to make the same recipe for a bigger cake. If you use 4 cups of butter, how much sugar will you need to use? Draw a picture or use numbers to show how you figured it out.

Q. Make up a problem using this same recipe for a *very large* cake. Explain how much butter and how much sugar you would need for *your* cake.

Ratio Task #2

Q. A scale model of a house is 1 foot high. The scale is 1:30 or $\frac{1}{30}$. How high is the real house? On the board, draw the house one foot high.

Q. On the same scale, a model tree is 2 feet high. In your picture on the board, draw the tree 2 feet high. How high is the real tree?

Q. On the same scale, about how tall would a model of *you* be? Draw yourself to scale in your picture.

Percents

Percents are ratios, too. 60% means $\frac{60}{100}$. Percents help us compare ratios to each other. 60% is a larger ratio than 40%. Percents communicate ratio well because we are so familiar with the numbers from 1 to 100. $\frac{60}{100}$ is much more meaningful to most people than $\frac{90}{150}$ even though they both refer to the same ratio.

Here are some tasks involving percents.

Percent Task #1

A weather report on the radio makes a correct prediction 45% of the time.

Q. Is this good enough? What do you think? Explain your answer.

Q. Is the weather prediction correct more or less than half the time?

Q. Why do you think the prediction is not correct 100% of the time? What do you think would be a reasonable percent for a correct weather report prediction?

Percent Task #2

Q. About what percent of every 24 hours do you spend asleep? On a school day, about what percent of every 24 hours do you spend in school? About what percent do you spend watching television? What percent do you spend eating? Do all those hours add up to 100%? If not, what else do you do during the day?

Q. Tell how you figured out what percent of the 24 hours you spend asleep.

Q. Which do you spend more time doing, sleeping or attending school?

Q. What percent of the 24-hour day do you spend at your favorite activity?

Other Percent Tasks

Q. Write 75% as a fraction. How do you write a percent as a fraction? How are fractions and percents alike? How may they be different?

Q. Write the fractions as percents: $\frac{1}{2}$, $\frac{3}{4}$, $\frac{9}{10}$, $\frac{85}{100}$. Based on your results, can you arrange those four fractions in order, from least to greatest? How do you change a fraction to a percent? How can you tell which percent is the greatest?

▲ Decimals

Decimal numbers are a logical extension of the place value system that we use for whole numbers. Each position to the right has a value equal to $\frac{1}{10}$ of the value of its neighbor to the left, just as is the case for whole numbers. The difference is that to the right of the decimal point, a digit has a value which is less than one. To the left of the decimal point, each digit has a value that is equal to or greater than 1.

The decimal point itself is just a marker between the whole numbers and the fractions. It is more meaningful to students if teachers avoid using the word *point* when naming numbers. When you ask the following questions, try to read .5 as "five-tenths" rather than "point five."

Decimal Task #1

Q. Arrange in order from least to greatest:

.5   .09   .16   5.1

Explain how you did it.

Q. How can you tell which of two decimal numbers is greater than the other one?

Q. Someone said that .09 is greater than .5 because 9 is greater than 5. Could he be right? If he is right, show how you know that. If he is not right, explain how you could help him understand his mistake.

Decimal Task #2

Ask your students to write the following numbers as fractions:

.6   .26   .314   .048   1.03

Q. In each case, how did you decide what number to use as a denominator?

Q. How would you explain to a friend how to write a decimal as a fraction?

Q. Which is easier, changing a fraction to a decimal or changing a decimal to a fraction? Explain why.

Other Decimal Tasks

Q. Read (write) the following:

1.5   6.12   9.03

Q. School supplies cost:

pencil: $.15   eraser: $.20   notebook: $1.25

How much would it cost to buy 3 pencils, an eraser, and 2 notebooks?

Q. How would you explain to a second grader what the decimal point is for in writing $2.35? How would you explain to a second grader what the decimal point is for in writing the number 2.35?

Q. Add:

.1 + .03 + 2.5 + 1.25

Explain how you did it.

Q. What is a mixed numeral? For each of the following numbers, tell which part represents a whole number and which part represents a fraction:

1.3   6.75   12.07

Write the numbers as mixed numerals.

Q. Read (write):

.132   .0092   .00005   .000004

Q. Multiply:

1.7 × .4   .6 × 750   .03 × .007

For each problem, explain how you decided where to put the decimal point in your answer.

Q. Divide 6 by 1.5 and use multiplication to check your work.

Q. Use mental math to multiply:

6.4×10 6.4×100 $6.4 \times 1,000$

How did you get your answers? How did you decide where to put the decimal point in your answers?

Q. Use mental math to divide:

$5.2 \div 10$ $5.2 \div 100$ $5.2 \div 1,000$

How did you get your answers?

Q. Estimate which is larger:

6.5×10 or $.05 \times 100$

How did you do it? Use a calculator to see whether you are correct. Were you correct? If not, what was your mistake?

▲ Geometry

Geometry is of increasing importance in the elementary curriculum. Some important big ideas have to do with classification and naming of different shapes, their properties, and their distinguishing features. Other big ideas have to do with distance, area, and volume and their measurement. Important vocabulary includes words that are difficult for some children, such as *inside, outside, between, similar,* and *congruent.*

Geometry Task #1
This first task involves names and properties of shapes. It can be adapted easily to any shape—square, triangle, rectangle, and so on. Do not let a child's difficulty with drawing interfere with success in this task. The object is not that the child draw perfectly. The object is to discover what the child knows about shapes. In a square, for example, all of the sides are equal in length, the square has four corners (or angles or vertices), all four vertices are equal, they each measure 90°, the sides are perpendicular and parallel to each other, the square is a closed figure, all squares are similar in shape, some square objects are tiles, blocks, boxes, pattern blocks, and so forth.

Q. What is the name of this shape? [*Pointing to a square, for example*] How do you know that it's a square? [*Pointing to additional shapes including some squares and some other shapes*] Is this a square too? Is this? How do you know it's (it's not) a square? Can you draw a square? What did you think while you were drawing your square? What do you have to be careful about when you draw a square? Can you find something square in this room?

Geometry Task #2

There are many ways to find the area of a rectangular sheet of paper. Try to discover whether the student understands the concepts of area and area units of measure. The students should have available a standard ruler and one-inch blocks or a metric ruler and centimeter blocks, tiles, pen or pencil, and scratch paper. Notice whether the student uses the ruler, tiles, or other objects of known measurement. Notice, too, whether the student uses correct units of measure: *square* inches or *square* centimeters, for example.

Q. How could you find the area of this sheet of paper? Do it and tell me your result. Use any tools or materials that you need.

Q. How could you check your result?

Q. Can you show me how much is one square inch (centimeter)?

Q. Is there another way to find the area of the paper? Do it.

Q. Which way do you like better? Why?

Q. Can you draw a rectangle that has an area of 12 square inches (centimeters)? How do you know that your rectangle has an area of 12 square inches (centimeters)?

As an extension of this task, ask students to estimate the area of a shape other than a rectangle, such as a triangle, a circle, or an irregular shape. Ask them to explain their strategies.

Geometry Task #3

Words that describe relations between objects often are difficult for children. There are standardized tests to assess understanding of those concepts, but you can invent your own tasks just as well. Ask the student questions about objects in the classroom.

Q. What is under the reading table? Whose desk is closest to the clock? Who sits between Jamie and Richard? Which is the highest picture on that wall?

Q. Pretend that I cannot find the wastebasket (the clock, the chalk-tray, my desk). Tell me exactly where it is.

Q. Pretend that you are an ant just crawling over the doorsill into the room. How would you tell your ant friend how to get to those lunch scraps in the wastebasket?

Q. Pretend that you are a bird flying in at the door. How would you tell your bird friend how to get to that open window?

Other Geometry Tasks

Q. Estimate which of these empty boxes would hold more sand. How could you see whether your estimation was correct?

Q. Sort these cardboard triangles into three piles: equilateral, isosceles, and scalene. For each one, explain how you decided which pile to put it in.

Q. [*Draw a picture of several angles of different sizes.*]

Which of these angles is the smallest? How can you tell?

Which of these angles are greater than 90°?

Estimate the measure of each of these angles. Explain your thinking.

Q. Which has a greater area for playing, a playground that is 200 × 300 feet, or one that is 250 × 245 feet? How long a fence would be needed to surround each one? Does the playground with the larger area require a longer fence? Can you explain your answer?

▲ What Comes Next?

Now that you have read this chapter, you probably have some ideas of your own about questions that you would like to ask your students. To be successful, first focus your attention on exactly what it is that you are trying to find out about one of the students in your class. What big idea is involved? Then phrase your question in a way that will be just right for that particular student. Be sure to follow up your first question by asking the student to explain his or her thinking process. You may be surprised to find out how much you learn. Good luck!

CHAPTER EIGHT

▲ *What Teachers Say about Using Flexible Interviewing in the Classroom*

Teachers have told us that using flexible interviewing in the classroom involves more than just the application of a technique. Indeed, the use of flexible interviewing leads to a transformation of teachers' beliefs about teaching and learning.

As you know, we carried out our project with teachers from public and private schools in New York and in suburban Connecticut, working together to find ways to implement flexible interviewing in the classroom. From the beginning, some teachers already believed that it is more interesting and important to gain insight into the child's thinking than to record the number of correct and incorrect answers. A few already had used interviewing techniques with their students.

At the end of our work, we asked the participating teachers to tell us what their experience with flexible interviewing during the project had meant to them as teachers. They told us that using individual and group flexible interviewing allowed them to investigate the thought processes underlying their students' answers. These changes in the way teachers assessed their students led to a new and different understanding of student learning, of mathematics, and consequently of their own teaching.

Teachers' accounts made it clear that learning to do flexible interviewing is not just a matter of learning how to ask good questions. The use of flexible interviewing involves a transformation of the teachers' conceptual view of what they believe children really know and can do. That transformation took different forms. Here are some of the ways in which teachers changed their views about assessment, about teaching mathematics, and about children's mathematical knowledge.

▲ Assessment Practices

Teachers' accounts expressed their lack of satisfaction with traditional standardized, criterion-referenced, timed testing. Their experience with flexible interviewing helped them to move away from that tradition of assessing by counting right and wrong answers. They came to view assessment as a tool to help them understand and foster students' thinking.

The use of interviewing brought about other notable changes in teachers' views and practices. For instance, assessment became a part of their daily teaching experiences. Often, teachers avoided assigning special times for assessing students. Instead, they integrated assessment into their daily plans for instruction. Teachers also began to see that there is a close link between assessment and learning. They discovered that while students are being assessed, they are also learning, developing their thinking, and developing their ability to reflect on what they do and know. In this way, teachers' new views of assessment began to make an impact on the way they were teaching.

Assessing and Fostering Thinking in the Classroom Becomes a Routine

Let's read next some accounts about how teachers evaluated the experience of interviewing. We will begin by discussing what Thomas had to say:

> The experience I have acquired from this has been valuable. I think that kids have gotten a lot from it, because I have gotten to know them better. It has made a difference in how I teach them. You can get a more on-target evaluation of kids. The whole idea of inquiry I believe was ideal. I think students' thinking has improved. There were a lot of benefits for the kids. I think that process is the way to do math.

Clearly Thomas is aware of the impact that flexible interviewing has had not only on his views and assessment practices, but also upon his teaching. It is very interesting as well to see how sensitive he has been to his students' experience. He notes that flexible interviewing has been productive and positive for them too.

Finally, as we can see from Thomas's comment, "process is the way to do math," his view of mathematics has broadened to include student thinking as a major focus of the curriculum.

Clara expressed her new perspective about assessment when she said:

> I am fighting with whether I should continue to give these timed tests. Is it really necessary?

One of Clara's students, a third grader, was so fast at timed tests that he dazzled the other children. It amazed them that a child actually could complete the test within the time limit. Clara was concerned that while some children love the challenge of a timed test, others fear it. She said that sometimes she thinks she should offer it only as an optional activity for those who wish to do it.

Let's take a look at what Dan and Susan had to say about their experiences with assessment. Dan said:

> I have changed as a teacher with this project. I question kids more. More and more kids are asking questions too. Maybe they know I will ask questions, so they are getting prepared. They are all sharing the ideas.

In line with Dan's comments, Susan added:

> It becomes a natural process. I am doing it where I am. I don't even feel that I'm doing it. I think it gives me a truer understanding of how important it is to talk to a child. I feel that I get to know the children very well.

Susan's and Dan's experiences show that assessment has become an integral part of their instruction. They value students' ability to question and talk about their thinking, because it allows the teacher to get to know much better what students understand about mathematics.

It is important to note that in the accounts of these teachers there is a sense of a positive achievement that they feel good about. This is true of most, if not all, of the teachers with whom we worked. Their experience with flexible interviewing was gratifying, and gave most of them a feeling of security in their teaching.

In sum, the teachers reconsidered their approach to assessment. They developed the view that questioning and the assessment of thinking and of understanding take precedence over the traditional, standardized, right-and-wrong-answer approach. They came to believe in the utility of embedding questioning within the process of teaching because they discovered that children learn a great deal from the process of interviewing itself.

▲ Teaching Practice, Views of Learning, and Views on What the Teaching of Mathematics Is All About

Teachers also indicated that they had changed their views about how the teaching and learning of mathematics take place.

The majority of the teachers felt that interviewing changed their teaching practices away from direct instruction and toward a more constructivist approach. They changed their beliefs about how learning takes place. They moved away from viewing the student as a passive receptor of information and toward a view of the student as an active participant in the learning process. They moved away from telling the student *what* to do and *how* to do it, and toward guiding students to construct their own knowledge.

Within this framework, they began to see that children learn from their experiences as they interact with one another. They observed their students constructing new concepts in order to restore coherence and meaning to their beliefs. The changes in teachers' views about how children learn had an impact upon their views about mathematics instruction.

Moving from Worksheets and Workbooks to Cooperative Learning and the Use of Manipulatives

Let's read next what teachers had to say about how they changed their teaching methods. We will begin by discussing what Nina had to say about moving from worksheets and workbooks to cooperative learning and the use of manipulatives. Nina said:

Rather than giving worksheets and workbooks, one thing I have been doing a lot of this year is a math problem of the day. It is interesting to look at the different ways they work, and we emphasize that.

Now Nina's students work in cooperative learning groups. She observes her students' written and drawn strategies, notes how they use manipulatives, how they collaborate, and how they discuss the problems.

Notice in Nina's account that changing her beliefs about how children learn led her to move away from traditional seatwork and toward the use of cooperative learning. As her students developed their thinking skills together, Nina had opportunities to observe them. Her observations provided her with rich data about her students' thinking and understanding.

Other teachers who made the change toward cooperative learning groups came to see mathematics differently and have enjoyed the new approach. For instance, Margaret said:

> The major change is that I now teach a cooperative group and I evaluate as I'm teaching. It's a group interview. It's made me much more comfortable with math. Where other years I would say, "Oh, oh, I haven't done any math," you know, and I'd have to kind of suddenly fit it in, now it is a rare day that I don't get to math.

It is important to pay special attention to the fact that Margaret turned cooperative learning groups into group interviews. Once students are able to work cooperatively, a group interview is not difficult to conduct. Often a task is broken down or divided among students in a cooperative group. Each student in a group may find it easier to talk about his or her particular role within that group than to talk about the entire task.

Other teachers made connections with different aspects of the curriculum.

Integrating Methods of Instruction across the Curriculum

Lucy was one of the teachers who brought up the issue of integrating methods of instruction across the curriculum. She had learned about student journals at a language arts workshop. Lucy began to ask her students to keep math journals and to record their thoughts. She sees clearly the relevance of what works in one curriculum area for other areas.

Emphasizing Students' Verbalizing of Their Thinking

Teachers changed their methods of instruction in many ways. Perhaps what teachers changed the most was the level of student participation in their classrooms. Clara, for example, is making sure that she gives students enough opportunities to talk about their strategies and give a rationale for them. With regard to her goals for future practice, Clara said:

> I think this work has opened my eyes; children should provide their own ways and justify their thinking.

The majority of the teachers participating in the project not only made the verbalization of children's thinking a goal, but actually began to reflect that goal in their practice right away, on a daily basis, as a part of their regular instruction.

Moving from Drill and Rote Learning to Teaching for Understanding

Moving from drill and rote learning to an emphasis on understanding, sharing of strategies, and verbalization of thinking was one of the most significant changes for many teachers. Most of them found a way to feel comfortable with this change. For others, however, it was not so easy. Let's read their accounts.

Lori still insists on the importance of rote learning and drill. Her third graders use the varied strategies that they learned in second grade. In mental subtraction, 15 – 7, for example, they use finger counting, counting down, related facts, and a two-step process using rounding. Lori, however, is upset with the variety of strategies and the lack of speed. She says:

> I never saw that before with third graders. They just knew it. I'm sure there are many adults who do it that way, so you know . . . but it's troublesome, somehow. Part of me is troubled by just seeing them use their fingers and not knowing the facts. I am sort of toying with it and fighting with it. I'm trying to decide whether it's O.K. and not to bother with it and not to say a word. My tendency is just to let them get the answer in any way they can, but I think it just bogs them down. My own kids were drilled in them [the facts] and they knew them, and they loved them. I think it is always important to teach things so that kids understand them. I use lots of problem solving and talking about why things work, but I think there comes a point . . . hopefully the time will come when they can just do these things more efficiently.

Kaila also had an important comment about rote learning and thinking. She said:

> . . . But the third-grade teachers are hard to convince that thinking can ever replace rote learning as preparation for standardized testing.

As we have said before, Lori's account reflects the concern of many teachers. It is true that both understanding and drill are important. One probably should precede the other, while the teacher maintains a healthy balance between the two. Once understanding is in place, drill and rote learning can provide the speed for efficient problem solving.

Moving from Direct Instruction to Constructivist Learning

Teachers were deeply concerned about a related issue that they felt was crucial to their teaching: the balance between direct instruction and a more cognitive approach. Several accounts will illustrate their thinking.

Kaila, who is the math coordinator for a lower school, and therefore concerned with more than just her own classroom, said:

> What's an issue now, is how to carry over and how to make this keep going. When I talk to teachers in the fourth grade and the fifth grade, the children get so hung up on algorithms that they give up their strategies. They give up their thinking skills. At a meeting, the third grade teachers asked, "When do we teach borrowing? When do we teach carrying?" because it is not written down.

Kaila argues that if children have enough work with manipulatives, they naturally go to grouping by tens. Moreover, there is always someone who has learned from a parent or older brother or sister and who shows the rest of the class how to borrow or carry. She says:

> It just comes naturally.

Flora became aware of her tendency to tell students what to do or how to solve problems, rather than letting the students figure out for themselves what to do. She said that this was due to her tendency to protect her students. Flora explained:

For some reason, probably because I am concerned when just a few kids don't get it, I tend to give away too much information, rather than questioning and having the children be more involved in helping each other. I am learning to let them do it. I lay back more and more and become a facilitator.

In a similar vein, Dan acknowledged:

I give kids the answers. I get very uncomfortable when kids don't know some information. Silence makes me nervous, so I make statements and give conclusions.

Thomas agreed:

I find it difficult not to "tell" or "teach" my students the concepts. I find that the instruction is a better use of my time. Assessment is part of what you should do, but you should move on.

In the case of rote learning versus learning with understanding, a healthy balance between direct instruction and cognitive learning is a good idea. There is always a time and a place for direct instruction. Children do need to construct their own learning, but in some situations students also need the specific guidelines that direct instruction can provide.

Moving from Product to Process

Teachers worked to make a shift away from a product-oriented approach with its emphasis on right and wrong answers to a more process-oriented approach emphasizing thinking, processing, and strategies. Martha noticed that such a shift was difficult not only for some teachers but also for many students as well:

For students to shift was very difficult. At the beginning they resisted strongly. They wanted to know if they were right or wrong.

Martha expressed it this way:

It was very difficult for students to accept the importance of thinking. Some did accept it. One student said, "I don't see the point of stretching our mind. Tell me what is wrong to change it." Toward the end of our work, students were much more comfortable with the work and listened to each other.

Similarly, Dan found it difficult for his students to accept the shift from product to process. They were more interested in right and wrong answers than in their strategies.

Dan also indicated that the initial sessions were rough on students. They needed to learn to focus on strategies rather than on answers. They also needed to learn how to write about their thinking. Once these skills began to develop, students felt much more comfortable with the work.

Thomas was accustomed to correcting students' wrong answers immediately rather than giving students an opportunity to find their errors themselves. Making a shift from product to process required Thomas to change this practice. He describes the initial discomfort that he experienced this way:

> Working in the project made me aware of the tendency to ignore wrong answers or to tell students right away that they were wrong, without giving them the opportunity to think. In order to avoid interpreting or making inferences about what kids were saying, I had to keep biting my lips. When we started the project I thought I would not feel comfortable working like this all the time. I have a tendency to turn my classes into more teacher-directed instruction. As the project comes to an end, I am not feeling the need to bite my tongue. The key to it is to create a balance between direct instruction and alternative assessment.

Thomas's last remark is quite valuable. It is important to keep a balance between an emphasis on product and on process. Teachers accustomed to focusing on right and wrong answers cannot reasonably be asked to ignore product altogether. Rather, as they learn to attend to their students' thinking processes, they may use questioning and interviewing to get at both the correctness of the responses and the thinking underlying those responses.

Moving from Passive, Receptive Learning to Active Learning

Another important change for many teachers was that of teaching children to become active participants in the classroom. It was not an easy task. It required time and effort. Margaret, for example, said that now she is giving students the opportunity to talk about their feelings when they do the group interviews. She also is giving them the chance to make decisions about seating arrangements when they are going to do math work. She said:

We also have to give the kids time to talk about how they feel and let them make decisions. If they are involved they feel part of the team. They did not feel that way before. Now they help me clean up without having been asked, which makes me feel better.

Relinquishing the Authority in the Classroom

When teachers change their beliefs about instruction and learning, the result is a change in the atmosphere of the classroom. As teachers in our project changed their beliefs, one of the most significant results was that the teacher began to share with students the authority and the responsibility for thinking. The teacher is no longer the official source of right answers. Clara's comments refer to this effect when she says:

> Since children provide their own explanations and achieve a consensus about answers, I do not need to offer answers or official solutions to problems. I am no longer the authority and source of knowledge whose role is to transmit information. In order to get students thinking, I had to change my attitude about how I teach. I am not giving the answers. This forced the children to take the responsibility of figuring it out themselves.

Lucy also emphasizes that she adapts her instruction to students' needs on the basis of what they write in their journals. Lucy said:

> Every once in a while, when you look at the journal, you see that they misunderstood something that you thought they did understand. But I have to teach them again.

So Lucy's and Clara's curriculum is guided by students' needs. They feel responsible for reteaching whenever necessary.

The accounts just reviewed show that teachers' changed beliefs about teaching and learning brought about changes in the teaching of mathematics, leading to the development of a more thinking-oriented classroom than had existed before. Flexible interviewing clearly had an impact on the way they view their role as teachers and their students' role as learners.

▲ *Teacher Beliefs about Students' Knowledge*

Teachers also commented about changes in how much students knew about mathematics. Let's take a look at this issue next.

The use of flexible interviewing led several teachers to realize that it offers a way to discover valuable but unexpected information about what their students actually know and understand. Teachers were surprised to find that some students who give the appearance of understanding really had important misconceptions and needed further instruction.

Other students who really did have the basis of excellent conceptual understanding had not revealed the depth of their understanding in class or on a test. Many teachers were excited by the complexity and variety of student responses to questioning. That variety was in stark contrast to the relative uniformity of answers given on paper and pencil tests. As Anna put it:

> He is a quiet, delicate child. I had no idea what he would do. He counted pennies by 4's, then decided that counting by 10's was easier. He arranged pennies in stacks of 10, not a usual strategy in this class. He checked the heights of the stacks and evened them up when one was a penny short. He reversed the digits of written numbers but could write numbers up to 99. He knew that 47 and 3 more pennies would make 50. He could count by 2's, 3's, and 10's. The interview was interrupted by rhythms class. He said, "I hate rhythms. I get headaches."

Anna was quite surprised by how much she was able to learn about this child in a short time. His ability with numbers was far greater than she had anticipated.

She characterized another quiet child:

> He lacks confidence. He is hard to write a report about. He is in the middle. He does not verbalize or stand out.

During an interview with him, Anna was surprised by his consistently strong skills and understanding.

She said:

> He's stronger than I thought.

Along the same lines, Tara said:

> I often overestimate what my students know. I have the tendency to put a filter coat on right answers. I think I know my students' thinking, and yet, at the end I am usually surprised.

Tara said that she now had a more accurate view of her students' understanding of the concept of exchange (borrowing or carrying). She was surprised with the insight and clever understanding displayed by some of the students who she thought were not comprehending. On the other hand, two of the students who she thought were doing well were unable to display a complete understanding of the exchange process.

Teachers' accounts continued to highlight how much they could learn about their students. Often a teacher has a problem student, one who is a mystery to the teacher. After interviewing one of her first-grade "problem students," Lisa announced that she was "thrilled by the results." She had just sent out grades to parents, with a rather poor report for that child. She planned to give the mother a phone call with positive comments about the strengths she had newly discovered in the child's mathematical understanding. She planned to design further instruction to help the child build upon those strengths.

In our final example, Nina, already a skilled interviewer, was accustomed to interviewing each of her kindergarten students in preparation for the first parent conference of the year. Here is what she reported:

> The one thing that sort of took me by surprise is the amount of growth of the students from June until September with some students, particularly noticing some of the ones that I had in kindergarten last year. I had a couple of children, not that they struggled through kindergarten, but they were sort of plodding along and making steady progress. I knew where they were in June and all of a sudden September came. When I sat down to do the first round of conference interviews I kept saying, "Wait a minute, did you get tutored over the summer? Did you go to summer school?"

The change in the quality of her students' understanding was so marked that these children, with whom she was so familiar, surprised Nina greatly. Even at a time in the school year when children may have forgotten much during the summer, they seemed to have learned even more.

Not only in the summer do children learn math out of school. Informal math skills are developed through everyday experiences. The teacher can use flexible interviews to discover those unexpected strengths in students. The knowledge gained helps the teacher in planning further instruction.

The accounts shared by participating teachers have shown how valuable a tool flexible interviewing can be. Through the use of questions that assess thinking, teachers were often surprised to discover their students' true level of understanding of mathematical concepts. Most of the surprises were positive. Students usually knew more than their teachers had realized.

▲ Conclusion

In this chapter we have seen that the use of flexible interviewing in the classroom helps teachers to develop instruction that is compatible with a constructivist perspective. Teachers commented on the impact that flexible interviewing had on their assessment and teaching practices as well as their beliefs about how children learn. Without throwing out the best of traditional instruction practices, they learned to make their classrooms more thinking-oriented.

Teachers talked about how they altered their teaching techniques to provide learning opportunities that encourage students to construct their own learning. They allowed their students' interests and needs to help determine the curriculum.

They learned to be better questioners and better listeners. They helped their students learn to share problem-solving strategies, to assess their own thinking, to value thinking processes as well as just the right answers, and to take responsibility for their own learning.

Finally, teachers and students shifted toward a recognition that what may seem like errors and confusion are merely children's expressions of their current understanding. Assessment became for many teachers a creative activity that invites teachers and students to join in an exciting dialogue.

It can be your dialogue too.

▲ *References*

Baroody, A. J. (in press). Fostering children's mathematical power: An investigative approach to K–8 mathematics instruction. Columbus, OH: Merrill/Prentice Hall.

Binet, A., & Simon, T. (1916). *The development of intelligence in children.* Baltimore, MD: Williams & Wilkins.

Ginsburg, H. P. (1989). *Children's arithmetic: How they learn it and how you teach it* (2nd ed.). Austin, TX: Pro Ed.

Ginsburg, H. P. (1998). *Entering the child's mind: The clinical interview in psychological research and practice.* New York: Cambridge University Press.

Ginsburg, H. P., & Baron, J. (1992). Cognition: Young children's construction of mathematics. In R. J. Jensen (Ed.), *Research ideas for the classroom: Early childhood education* (pp. 3–21). New York: Macmillan.

Ginsburg, H. P., & Opper, S. (1988). *Piaget's theory of intellectual development* (3rd ed.). Englewood Cliffs, NJ: Prentice-Hall.

National Council of Teachers of Mathematics. (1995). *Assessment standards for school mathematics.* Reston, VA: Author.

Piaget, J. (1973). *To understand is to invent: The future of education* (G. Roberts & A. Roberts, Trans.). New York: Grossman.

Piaget, J. (1976). *The child's conception of the world* (J. Tomlinson & A. Tomlinson, Trans.). Totowa, NJ: Littlefield, Adams.

Stevenson, H. W., & Stigler, J. W. (1992). *The learning gap: Why our schools are failing and what we can learn from Japanese and Chinese education.* New York: Summit.

Wainer, H. (1992). *Measurement problems* (Program Statistics Research No. 92-12). Princeton, NJ: Educational Testing Service.

▲ *Index*